My Passage from India

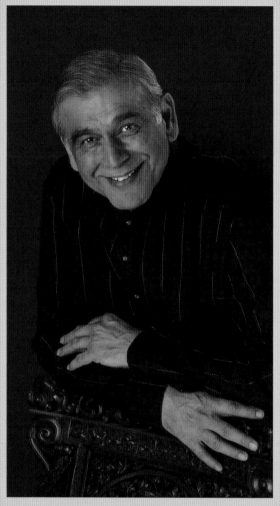

My Passage from India

A FILMMAKER'S JOURNEY

FROM BOMBAY TO HOLLYWOOD

AND BEYOND

Ismail Merchant

Viking Studio

Viking Studio
Published by the Penguin Group
Penguin Putnam Inc., 375 Hudson Street,
New York, New York 10014, U.S.A.
Penguin Books Ltd, 80 Strand,
London WC2R 0RL, England
Penguin Books Australia Ltd, 250 Camberwell Road, Camberwell,
Victoria 3124, Australia
Penguin Books Canada Ltd, 10 Alcorn Avenue,
Toronto, Ontario, Canada M4V 3B2
Penguin Books India (P) Ltd, 11 Community Centre, Panchsheel Park,
New Delhi – 110 017, India
Penguin Books (N.Z.) Ltd, Cnr Rosedale and Airborne Roads, Albany,
Auckland, New Zealand
Penguin Books (South Africa) (Pty) Ltd, 24 Sturdee Avenue,
Rosebank, Johannesburg, 2196, South Africa

Penguin Books Ltd, Registered Offices:
Harmondsworth, Middlesex, England

First published in 2002 by Viking Studio,
a member of Penguin Putnam Inc.

1 3 5 7 9 10 8 6 4 2

CIP data available

ISBN 0-670-03163-1

This book is printed on acid-free paper.

Printed in England
Set in Weiss
Designed by Jaye Zimet

For Jim,

without whom this journey
would not have been possible

Acknowledgments

I would like to acknowledge with gratitude the invaluable contribution of Anna Kythreotis, who has helped to shape this manuscript; my astute and helpful editor Adrian Zackheim; and Chris Terrio and Corey Hajim for working with the photos and graphics printed here as I continue to fly from continent to continent. I am grateful to Cyrus Jhabvala, for his vigilance and attention to detail. I would also like to thank my dear friend Clare Ferraro, who has commissioned this book from a one-page outline. Finally, I am grateful to the many wonderful photographers who have captured this story in images over the years including Anna Kythreotis, Douglas Webb, Karan Kapoor, Seth Rubin, Parveena Hafizka, Tara Poda Banerjee, John Swope, Mikki Ansin, Mary Ellen Mark and Christopher Cormack.

Introduction

One evening forty years ago James Ivory and I sat in a coffee shop, the Right Bank on Madison Avenue in New York, and discussed the idea of making Indian-themed films for an international audience. Recently I was told that a plaque would be erected on the site to mark the place where the Merchant Ivory partnership began.

It occurred to me that a whole generation of film audiences have grown up since that time knowing Merchant Ivory only for the period adaptations with which we are now associated. And yet, long before we made a name for ourselves in that particular niche, we had spent almost twenty years exploring and refining our craft on films based in present-day India. Overshadowed and perhaps eclipsed by our recent successes, those Indian films established both the themes and the style of our entire body of work.

India is my country: the place which ignited my passion for film, and where my adventures as a filmmaker started.

My Passage from India

I can remember the exact moment when I knew that I wanted to spend my life in the world of movies. I was thirteen years old and had been invited by Nimmi, one of the upcoming stars in the Bombay film industry, to accompany her to the premiere of her first film, *Barsaat*. As we drove toward the cinema in her green Cadillac convertible—quite an impressive car in India at that time—a shower of marigolds began to rain down on us. I looked up, and it seemed as though the marigolds were dropping from the night sky—thousands of golden flowers gently falling around us. By the time we emerged, the open car was full of marigolds—and still they fell as we walked into the cinema, scattering petals along the way, as crowds of people stared and called out Nimmi's name. It is customary in India to greet guests and important people with garlands of marigolds, but I had never seen it done like this, or on such a scale. It seemed so magical—like the movies themselves—that I can remember thinking, "If this is what the film world is, I want to be a part of it." I wanted to be involved in this fabulous life of applauding people and showers of marigolds. From that moment, my father's dreams for me to become a doctor or a lawyer were doomed.

Nimmi's family had a close friendship with my family. They had met at Ajmer in Rajasthan, the burial place of Khwaja Mohinuddin Chistie, a holy man—believed to have miraculous powers—whose shrine is a place of pilgrimage for both Muslims and Hindus. As my family's saint for over a century, it was to him that my mother went to pray for a son after the birth of three daughters. The good saint obliged, and I appeared on Christmas Day, 1936.

The premiere of *Barsaat* was the defining moment of my life: I became completely obsessed with movies—and with Nimmi. After school I would

After the completion of the film In Custody, *I traveled to Ajmer to get the blessing from our Saint Khwaja Mohinuddin Chistie. I was greeted by a local politician.*

R. K. Films

Nimmi, in Aan, one of her most successful films, was my earliest inspiration toward a career in film.

• • • • • • • •

Screen star Nimmi performs a song in Barsaat, *her first film.*

walk to her apartment house near Marine Drive and wait there on the doorstep for her to return from the studio. Nimmi lived with her grandmother, who accepted my presence, and from time to time there were other relatives and friends who visited from Agra and Dholpur. If Nimmi arrived home before me, I would be admitted to the apartment by one of the servants who looked after her, and be told to wait in the drawing room. Sometimes I would wait there for hours only to be told that Nimmi was too tired after working all day and would not be leaving her bedroom. When that happened, I would go home wretchedly miserable. Nimmi often took me to watch her shooting a film, and at other times we would go to the Eros cinema together to see English-language movies starring Susan Hayward, Bette Davis or Joan Crawford. We loved watching those larger-than-life Hollywood goddesses. When she came to visit us at our home in Bombay, crowds of people would gather in the street outside waiting for her to come out, and I felt very important for having such a huge star as a friend.

I understood nothing then of what film producers were or what they did, but having made up my mind that I wanted to spend my life in the magical

I introduce my childhood heroine Nimmi to Jeanne Moreau.

atmosphere of marigolds, I became impatient to grow up and get on with it. School was just a nuisance; I did enough work to pass from one grade to the next, but had no interest in achieving any sort of academic distinction. My father, alas, had different views. He was a textile dealer with the usual middle-class aspirations for his son, and he sent me to the best schools he could afford—from which, much to his fury when I got caught, I would sometimes play truant to watch a football or cricket match, or hang around Nimmi.

Little wonder then that I always keenly looked forward to the summer monsoon, not only because I enjoyed the sensation of getting drenched as I ran home—then drying off and changing into fresh clothes—but also, and more particularly, because our area would often be flooded and we couldn't go to school.

My favorite time of the year, though, was the spring, when schools would close for two months and we would go on holiday to Dewlali, a small hill station outside Bombay, or sometimes to Lonavla, the site of the Karla Caves created by Buddhist monks in the first century. But it wasn't the history or the cultural significance of the caves that drew me so much as the belief that they were haunted. Every time we went there I would go exploring in the caves, looking for ghosts, because I thought it might be interesting to confront a ghost. When I got tired of that, I would climb into a mango tree and gorge on the fat, juicy mangoes that were then coming into season.

Often, too, we would make a pilgrimage to Ajmer to pay tribute to our saint, Khwaja Mohinuddin Chistie: a practice my mother encouraged in me because of an episode there that convinced her I was particularly blessed. When I was a year old, my mother returned to the shrine and had me weighed in silver coins that were then distributed amongst the poor who wait at the shrine to receive alms. I was a strong, plump baby, so there would have been many coins to distribute. My mother told me that when she arrived at the shrine, a holy man was lamenting that no one was honoring the saint in the proper way, but when he saw us, he announced that a true disciple had arrived. It was my mother's wish, therefore, that I would be a *khadim*, a dedicated server of the saint. To this day, whenever I go to India, I make a special trip to Ajmer in order to observe the duties of a khadim. I buy baskets of roses and place them

An early portrait of me with my father, Noor Mohammed Merchant.

In Ajmer with flowers as an offering to the saint.

. . . .

The chaotic, sensual atmosphere of the Crawford Market in Bombay drew me as a child, and I return there on every trip to my home city.

Anna Kythreotis

on the shrine, and give alms to the poor and attend the evening prayers when a lantern of candles is placed on the head of each member of the congregation as a blessing. At *Urs*, the ten days that mark a celebration of the saint, the khadim sweep the vast area of the shrine with rosewater that is kept in leather pouches hung around their necks. In the evenings we sit under the trees and listen to the *allawalli* recite prayers to Allah, then to the *kawals* singing in praise of the saint. It was in Ajmer that we came to know

Nimmi and her family. So, for many reasons, this place continues to have a special significance for me.

When Nimmi left her home in Agra to pursue a movie career in Bombay, she often came to visit us. We lived in a small apartment in a Muslim neighborhood near Nul Bazaar, a noisy and colorful trading center known for the spice market run by Hindu shopkeepers. However, it was the Chinese lantern sellers who fascinated me most. Each of the Chinese women who made and sold these elaborate paper lanterns had a baby strapped to her back, and I wondered if the babies, too, were for sale. I would sit for hours watching the colored paper being made into fans and other shapes until the women grew tired of my gazing and finally shooed me away because I never bought anything. Equally intriguing were the Afghan traders, dressed in their distinctive embroidered jackets and white turbans, who peddled what can best be described as an Indian bazaar version of Viagra, an oily liquid in a bottle with a snake coiled in it—the original snake oil, presumably. This seemed to me a very unappealing product and, at the age of eight or nine, I simply couldn't understand the brisk trade it attracted. I was far more interested in acquiring my own elaborately embroidered Afghan jacket, baggy pants and turban.

Then there was Crawford Market, the vast fresh-produce market built in 1871 as a series of halls covering several blocks of downtown Bombay. The

cavernous interiors contain every imaginable food-stuff: meat, poultry, fish, towers of fruit and vegetables, exotic herbs and headily scented spices. Each stallholder competes with his neighbors to present the most attractive and colorful display, so the effect is like an endless picture gallery of exquisitely wrought still lifes. Tens of thousands of people come to shop here every day, creating a babel of hustle and bustle. The vast Victorian building is unique and has no real equivalent in the West, not even the old Covent Garden market in London or Les Halles in Paris before they were pulled down.

The absence of refrigeration in India made a visit to the market a daily necessity, and on days when there was no school I loved going there to amuse myself or just to look at the stalls and the people while my father selected our fresh meat, poultry, vegetables and fruit. Often we would have a fresh sherbet or a *faluda*, a kind of Indian milk shake, before returning home. Staples like rice and lentils and oil were delivered to the house once a month, but everything else was bought fresh from the market. Even today, and despite a huge refrigerator in my apartment in Bombay, buying fresh food daily is a habit we still follow, and Crawford Market is the first place I head for whenever I return to the city.

Long before I had an interest in cooking, I had developed an interest in eating, so as a boy I was a little on the chubby side—and still am. I was encouraged, therefore, to play hockey, volleyball and football at school, but my father was also keen that I should learn to swim and to ride, so every day in the

Karan Kapoor

summer months I would go with friends for swimming lessons to a pool near the sea at Back Bay. This involved a trolley ride that we made all the more exciting by jumping onto the fast-running cars then jumping off, or onto the second car, then back again in order to dodge the conductor. We had the money to pay our fare, of course, but this suicidal way of traveling seemed more fun. The possibility of being killed never occurred to me. I was far more fearful of being caught and reported to my parents, who knew nothing of my passion for joyriding and would have been appalled by these antics. As the only son in a family that eventually grew to six daughters, I was, inevitably, indulged—but I knew there were limits.

Every Saturday my father would go to the Turf Club for the horse racing. He was a passionate enthusiast of the sport and loved the excitement of betting. Often he would take me with him, and I would watch the proceedings with great fascination: the elegantly dressed members of Bombay's high society milling around the members' stand, the frantic business of placing bets, the excited yells of the winners. But I could never understand how

The Crawford Market in Bombay.

. . . .

The only boy in a family of seven children, in a recent photo with my six sisters (from left to right, front to back): Rashida, Amina, Saherbanoo, Saheeda, me, Rukhsana and Safiya.

people got such pleasure from a pursuit so riddled with anxiety, nor could I accept the idea of risking money on the skill of a jockey and the speed of a horse. When I started making movies, however, I realized that it was really no different from horse racing: It's just another form of gambling, although the torture is prolonged as you wait for a much longer time to see whether the film you have staked your money and your reputation on will be a winner.

A friend of my father's was an expert on form and he would pass on tips to my father while the horses were paraded in the ring before the start of each race. He was rarely wrong. He once tipped a horse called Chakori, an outsider, for a very big race. "If you think so," replied my father, who bet a substantial sum on the horse. Chakori won and my father made a killing. Luckily he put it away instead of losing it all in the next race.

Bombay was the focus of the racing season, which ran from December to March. Important races were also held in Pune, but my father never went to those because he disliked being away from his business interests, even though Pune was only a short distance from Bombay. Instead, he would ask his friends to take me along with them—something I was always keen to do, not because I had any interest in horse racing but because we always traveled there on the *Deccan Queen*, the fastest and best kept train on the whole Indian network.

Although I am like my father in many ways, I believe I have inherited something of my mother's character. She had a very open and generous nature, with a great gift for attracting people to her and making them feel welcome and at ease. She could strike up a conversation with anyone, and the house was always full of visitors who would never be allowed to leave until they had feasted on the wonderful food she prepared. Even her simplest meals were so delicious that no one could ever resist the invitation to stay for lunch or dinner—not that she would have allowed them to get away. She was also very adventurous, unusual for a woman in India at that time. She thought nothing of making the long trip to Ajmer on her own or with a female companion, rarely bothering to make a train reservation because she knew she could always depend on a conductor to find her a seat no matter how crowded the train was. She spoke very little English, and in such a funny way that we always teased her about it. I suppose the best compliment I can pay her is that all seven of her children relished her good company. But she had a quick temper, too, and I know I have inherited that: My passing rages, which once fell mostly on the kitchen help, are now legendary within the film community.

My mother indulged most of my whims, but she never allowed me to have a pet. I have a great affection for animals and would have loved to have had a dog, but because of rabies, dogs were considered unclean in Muslim households where prayers are conducted, so my mother never entertained the idea. My uncle, who was similarly prevented from having a guard dog, bought instead a parrot and had the brilliant notion of teaching it to say, "Chor! Chor!" which means "Thief! Thief!" Unfortunately, the parrot could not distinguish potential thieves from legitimate callers, so every guest was greeted with the cry "Thief! Thief!" This joke pleased my uncle no end.

Crawford Market was full of pets for sale, and I loved going there to see the animals and different kinds of birds. One day I saw a squirrel in a cage, and I liked it so much that I bought it. Nobody had said I couldn't have a squirrel. My mother was very concerned when she saw it, and insisted I get rid of it because squirrels bite. I explained to her that it was a pet squirrel, so it wouldn't bite. But when I released the squirrel from its cage, it jumped up and bit me. My mother was certain that I had been infected with rabies, and I was rushed to the hospital. This big drama seemed silly to me because I couldn't understand how anyone could die from a little squirrel bite. Even though the squirrel did not have rabies, I had to give it away.

The highlight of every year was the month of Ramadan, the annual thirty-day fast leading to the great celebration of *Idd*. Every day the family would rise at four to say prayers, and I remember a man chanting in the street, calling everyone to rise. After prayers we had a huge breakfast and that would be our only meal until sunset, when after evening prayers at the mosque, we would rush home for the *eftibari*, an equally huge evening meal by which we broke the fast. During Ramadan my maternal uncle Ibrahim

Essa would take me to a tailor to have a new suit made to wear at Idd, which marks the end of Ramadan. He chose only imported English fabric because it was the best, and I was always impressed by the way he could judge the quality of the material just by weighing it in his hand.

On the morning of Idd we would rise with the muezzin's call and walk to the mosque. The road on this occasion would be carpeted with white linen cloth for the hordes of people who were unable to get into the crowded mosque to say their Idd prayers. Then it was back home for a breakfast of sheer khorma, a wonderful milk-based dish with pistachios and almonds, decorated with gold or silver leaf. This dish is prepared and served at special occasions, such as Idd or weddings. For me, though, the very best part of the day was visiting friends and relatives who gave presents and money—rather like Christmas in the West. Because I was a son, I always seemed to get more money than my sisters, which made them very envious.

The five years following the end of the Second World War in 1945 were scarred by the riots and bloodshed of Indian partition in 1947, when India achieved its independence from British colonial rule and Pakistan was created as a separate Muslim state. Muslims and Hindus who had lived amiably side by side now became enemies. The Hindu spice sellers in our neighborhood, who had lived amongst us like brothers, also became victims of the indiscriminate attacks. This madness was incomprehensible to a child, and the violence and killings that became part of daily life left deep scars. Even today I have nightmares about the riots I witnessed in my neighborhood.

My family chose to remain in Bombay despite the violent situation prevailing in India. Bombay was our home and we had no intention of leaving or being forced to emigrate to another place. In 1945, as the disharmony and chaos began to gather momentum, some of the Muslim leaders from north and south of the country assembled in Bombay to discuss the position of Muslims in India. As president of the local Bombay branch of the Muslim League, my father was marginally involved in politics, and he had me memorize a speech written by a *maulvi*, a learned man and religious teacher, on the subject of partition. At the age of nine I barely understood the implications of what I was saying, but several thousand people, including all of my family, listened attentively as I addressed the gathering. The response was tumultuous—applause and cheers, and the crowd carried me on their shoulders at the conclusion of my speech. But politics was never likely to capture my heart.

Up until the age of fourteen I attended St. Joseph's, a Jesuit school, but my father also wanted me to learn Urdu and Persian, so I was then sent to Anjuman-i-Islam High School. That education helped me to appreciate the beautiful language of the great Urdu poets and writers.

I (far left) pose for a photo with Mohammed Ali Jinnah, the founder of the nation of Pakistan (seated, third from left). My father, Noor Mohammed Merchant, stands in the second row, sixth from left.

And my obsession with Nimmi, far from diminishing as I grew older, simply increased. I would go to the studios, uninvited, when she was filming and talk my way past the guards. I watched her as she sang for the cameras, imagining she directed her songs of love to me. A bad review for one of her films would send me into a furious rage, and I would vow revenge on the moronic critic who was clearly unqualified to practice his profession. Once, I got into a fistfight with some school friends who dared to suggest there were actresses better than she was.

Although my devotion to Nimmi was entirely innocent it was also very possessive. When I was fourteen, she began an affair with a cameraman and I became very jealous. I resented the man and the amount of time she sacrificed to him. Sometimes when I called at her apartment I would be told that Baby—everyone knew her as Baby—was out. But when I had seen her car parked in front of the apartment building, I would know she was in, probably entertaining the cameraman. So I would loiter in the hallway, and when he emerged from the apartment I would follow him to the elevator to make sure he left. Sometimes I even fantasized about beating him up.

When Nimmi's film *Aan* opened in London, she was invited to attend the premiere and the glittering reception that followed at the Savoy Hotel, hosted by the great British producer Alexander Korda. I felt totally bereaved during her absence from Bombay, and I have still not forgiven the English critic who wrote of that musical: "*Aan* is a film that goes aan and aan and aan." This was my first experience of film reviewers who often look for some element in a film to provide a joke at its expense.

I had joined the Metro Cub Club, which met every Sunday morning at the Metro cinema, a magnificent movie palace built in the 1930s, resplendent with marble staircases, glittering chandeliers and elaborate carpets. All the biggest MGM hits were shown there. On Sunday mornings I would take part in the music, singing and dancing program attended by students from schools and colleges in the Bombay area. But the films were what held the greatest fascination for me, and family outings to the cinema to watch the latest Bombay films were a great treat. For days afterward my sisters and

BFI

The scene from
Chandralekha
*that captured my
imagination.*

school friends and I would imitate the musical numbers and act out all
the dramatic scenes. I can still remember the impact these films had on
audiences. One film in particular, *Chandralekha*, was a huge musical-cum-
swashbuckling extravaganza with a spectacular finale that culminated in a
drum dance when the hero and his entire army emerge dramatically and, im-
probably, from hundreds of drums to fight the evil king and his soldiers. Far-
fetched it may have been, but people would return to the cinemas just to
watch the climactic scene over and over again.

On Saturdays and Sundays I would go with my closest friend, Karim
Samar, for a walk on Marine Drive, which overlooked the whole bay. Then
we would stop for coffee at Bombelli's, a Swiss coffee shop that made the
most sensational chocolate pastries. Sometimes we would walk to the Bori-
mohella district near the Chor Bazaar for the addictive cream puffs, like
cream-filled croissants, made by a Muslim sect called the Bora, or the fabulous ice cream they made from every kind of fresh fruit. At other times

Karim and I would save our pocket money and go to eat at Perk's or Gordon, which served European food: bland, often boiled, but nevertheless redolent of far-off sophisticated places. We also visited the Paiduni area, where all the food—from the kebabs to the nan bread—was studded with the fieriest chilies. Even as a teenager I was fascinated by other cultures: their lives, their cuisines and, of course, their cinema.

My family was very close to a family from Bareilly in Uttar Pradesh; one of their four sons, Hamed, was a great friend of mine. When the eldest son was to be married in Bareilly they invited me to go with them as a wedding guest. At that time I had never traveled beyond Bombay and the surrounding countryside where we took our holidays, so the chance of going to such a distant and exotic place seemed like a great adventure.

Bareilly lies to the west of Delhi, almost at the foothills of the lower Himalayan range. We arrived there at midnight after a long and exhausting train journey from Bombay. Regardless of the hour, the family in Bareilly had prepared a huge feast to welcome us, pressing more and more food on their hungry guests. At the center of this feast were some very special kebabs, their aromatic steam filling the night air as they were brought, hot and delicious, to the table. I fell on them like a hungry wolf, but with the first bite my ears popped, my eyes started to stream and my mouth felt as if it were on fire. Each kebab was stuffed with coriander and green chilies, and the green chilies of Uttar Pradesh are the hottest in the world. I had been warned that I would never forget those kebabs, and I never have. But they were so delicious that I kept on eating them, regardless of my streaming eyes, popping ears and the inferno they had made of my mouth, with the same enthusiasm that I enjoy the fiery food at a good Thai restaurant today.

Less than a hundred miles away was the town of Nainital, right on the edge of the Himalayas, close to a vast lake surrounded by English colonial summer houses. It was obvious why the English had chosen this lakeside spot as an escape from the fierce summer heat of the plains. It was so

beautiful that to me it seemed almost like paradise, and the air there was so fresh and clean that everything smelled new and somehow different. This had quite an impact on someone accustomed to the urban mayhem of Bombay.

Perhaps that trip stirred up some kind of wanderlust in me. Soon after returning to the city I was able to borrow Hamed's car and his driver and travel the 250 miles to Daman, near Goa, the Portuguese-held territory where European goods, especially perfumes and cosmetics, could be bought for a song. Two of my sisters, Safia and Amina, wanted to come with me, so we got into the car and took off on the long drive, keeping the whole adventure a secret from our parents.

Somewhere on an isolated stretch, the car broke down and we were stranded, miles from any town. In this deserted wilderness there was only a shabby little café on the side of the long dusty road. Years later I was reminded of this episode when I went to see the film *Baghdad Café*, which featured just such a place in an equally remote location that seemed so cut off as to have no connection with the rest of the universe. And that's certainly how we felt as we took shelter in the café, wondering if the driver could repair his engine and how we would ever get back to Bombay.

Eventually a bus heading for Bombay appeared and we got aboard, leaving the car with the driver. Our faces and hair were ashen with dust, and we were pallid with exhaustion by the time we returned, when I had to face the embarrassment of telling Hamed and his family what had happened, and try to make arrangements for someone to recover the car. Then I had to face my father. "What rabid dog has bitten you, that you should take off on such a crazy scheme?" he yelled. But I was sixteen years old, and it was one of those silly things one does in the buoyancy of youth. I had imagined filling the car with bottles of French perfume and other wonderful things to give our relatives and friends and, of course, boasting about the adventure.

I graduated from high school and, to my surprise, I was offered a place at St. Xavier's, the most exclusive and highly regarded college of Bombay University, to study for my B.A. degree. Run by the Jesuits, St. Xavier's was

no place for slackers. The college was very near the Metro cinema, and the other movie palaces were not far. I queued for hours to see *Gone With the Wind* at the Metro, and then it was the turn of Cecil B. DeMille's movies at the Empire cinema, especially *Samson and Delilah* and *The Ten Commandments*. Few European or art house movies were released in India, but I was able to see Yves Montand in *Wages of Fear*, and Kurosawa's *Rashomon*, both of which impressed me deeply.

From the beginning of my time at St. Xavier's, I was drawn to artistic rather than academic pursuits. I immediately joined—and soon became secretary of—the Sangeet Mandal, a music society which nurtured talented students through its variety programs. By a stroke of fortune, there were a number of gifted performers at St. Xavier's at that time, and we were frequently called on to represent the university on a national level.

Our first trip was to Delhi, a city I had never visited, which was hosting a student festival of all the Indian universities. After seeing the obligatory sights—the Red Fort and the Jamma Masjid—and having our photographs taken with the president of India, I was keen to meet students from the other universities to see what they were presenting. I was particularly interested in the students from Nagaland, who represented the University of Assam. Nagaland is inhabited by a variety of Tibeto-Burmese tribes, speaking more than twenty different dialects, who were once notorious headhunters. They offered our festival strange and hypnotic shuffling folk dances that I recalled many years later in America when I saw Native American tribal dances that seem to be cousins of these Naga performances.

The experience of meeting so many diverse people from different parts of India gave me an urge to travel, and that spring I decided to go to Kashmir. It was the first time I would be taking a true holiday on my own, and my family was not very enthusiastic about my going so far. But I wanted to see this beautiful part of India, so I boarded the train at Bombay for Pathankot, the last stop on the line. From there I had to travel by bus to my destination, Srinagar. On the day I arrived in Pathankot, however, a landslide had blocked the road and, typically, no one could tell us when it might reopen. It could

be a week, or a month. Unwilling to spend my vacation in Pathankot and determined to see Srinagar, I decided that no landslide was going to stop me.

I knew that light aircraft flew from Pathankot to Srinagar, but I had very little money. When I saw three American tourists waiting at the bus station who were also destined for Srinagar, I guessed that, unlike me, they were probably not strapped for cash. As we commiserated about the delay, I told them of the possibility of hiring a small plane and that if they were interested, I could negotiate a special deal for them provided I was allowed to be the fourth passenger on the flight, traveling free of charge. The deal was struck, and we went off to the little airstrip in search of a willing pilot.

Looking back, I can see that all the elements of my character, for which I have become infamous in the movie world, were apparent from my early years: impatience, stubbornness, guile, charm and, perhaps most notorious of all, the ability to part people from their money in order to achieve my own end. The trip to Kashmir demonstrated one of the earliest examples of this particular talent, which was to prove so useful in years to come.

The Mughal emperors who spent their summers in Kashmir described it as paradise, and no one since has come up with a better or more appropriate description for this enchanted landscape of mountains and valleys. It was like entering another world where even the people, with their fair hair, fair skin and blue eyes, looked unfamiliar. I sat in the shade of magnificent chinars, oriental plane trees, or wandered alongside brooks and trout streams and through lush orchards of apple, plum and almond trees, probably filing it all in my subconscious as a perfect film location, which, in fact, I would make use of some thirty years later in *Heat and Dust*. When we shot that film, the landscape was partially covered with snow, adding to the beauty of the film.

My return to Bombay was delayed by a series of mishaps—an accident somewhere on the track, a rerouting of the train, delayed arrivals and departures—and there was no way of telling my family that I would be back days later than expected. By the time I eventually arrived home the scene was like the final act of a Shakespearean tragedy, with much sobbing and wailing. My mother, her worst fears confirmed by my continuing absence, had already packed her bags and was ready to travel to the shrine at Ajmer to pray for me. She was so relieved and happy that I had not met some untimely end in the mountains that she prepared a feast that evening to celebrate my return. I was full of stories about what I had seen, the people I had met and the food I had eaten. I went into such raptures about the rice cooked with saffron on hot coals and the mincemeat with cream and almond sauce that I didn't notice my mother's growing vexation at my ingratitude for the feast she had prepared. I was released from my mother's anger when I gave her a beautiful shawl that I bought for her in Kashmir.

Now that I had discovered the perfect film location in Kashmir, I became very restless: I just wanted to get on and make movies (preferably with Nimmi as the star).

But in the meantime, I began to organize special events at the college—variety programs and fund-raising programs—and I even inaugurated an awards ceremony where bronze statuettes were given to outstanding students. While these kinds of events were not unusual—students were always putting on some sort of show—no one could match my productions in terms of scale and ambition. After all, I was connected with the Bombay film world. I had, by now, also introduced myself to the composers Shankar and Jaikishan, who worked as a team and were responsible for the music of many popular Hindi films, including those of the great star Raj Kapoor. Jaikishan, like Karim Samar and me, was also an habitué of Bombelli's, the Swiss café, where he would sit in a corner with his coffee and his tin of 555 cigarettes. I could not waste such an opportunity, so I introduced myself. Through him I could, and did, call on the services of some of the most famous playback singers in Bombay films, wheedling them into performing at our Sangeet Mandal shows.

I was also very enterprising when it came to selling advertising space in the programs for my shows. I would choose some of the most beautiful girls in the college and, in a borrowed car, we would pay calls on all the managing directors of the biggest companies in Bombay. We would turn up without appointments and just sit outside their offices. My function was to charm

the secretaries into letting us in, and once we were there, the combination of female beauty (the girls') and tenacious determination (mine) guaranteed a sale. Our mission accomplished, we would then go to a Chinese restaurant in the fort area to enjoy ourselves after our hard work. Each of us would contribute twenty rupees toward the meal until it occurred to me that there was actually no reason for us to pay at all. I proposed instead that we should take a percentage of the money paid for the advertisement as a cut for our work. No one argued against this idea.

By my third year of college I was putting together shows that perhaps, as I think about it now, were a portent of things to come. The scale of one of these was so ambitious—an eighty-piece orchestra and the greatest singers from the Bombay film world—that I felt it should be held in the college quadrangle. This imposing space was only used for religious services and College Day. It had never been given to any of the college societies for their functions, but perhaps no one else had badgered the authorities to the point where they had to agree if only to get rid of me. And perhaps no one really believed I would be able to pull off this grandiose scheme, not least because I had approached singers of the caliber of Lata Mangeskar, Mohammed Rafi and Manna Dey, who were the most famous playback singers from the Bombay film world. I couldn't pay them, so I decided to honor them: The occasion would be an awards ceremony where Bombay's finest students would honor the finest artists.

To inaugurate this event, I went to great lengths to engage the actress Nargis, then probably the biggest star in Indian films. Because I knew that everyone who came to these performances—students, their parents and members of the public—enjoyed watching these shows as much as I enjoyed organizing them, it never occurred to me that there might be some who resented the success of my activities, feeling perhaps that their own extracurricular efforts were overshadowed. So it came as a surprise to discover that one fellow student had maliciously tried to sabotage this event.

Just before the show was due to begin, some sixth sense prompted me to go to Nargis's home on Marine Drive, known as the Queen's Necklace, to

collect her rather than wait for her to arrive at the college, as had been previously arranged. Nargis had returned from the studio after shooting all day, and her manservant told me she was taking a bath before dinner. "But she is supposed to inaugurate our function tonight," I cried. With the minutes ticking away, I waited in the drawing room while Nargis finished her bath. She finally emerged with the explanation that somebody from my college had called earlier to tell her the show had been cancelled. I protested that it was just the opposite, that the musicians were probably striking up the overture at that very moment. Nargis didn't miss a beat. Within minutes she was dressed in her beautiful white sari, and we were speeding along the Queen's Necklace in her distinctive black-and-white Riley.

As we drove through the college gates I caught the eye of the likely saboteur, who until that moment had probably been thinking that Nargis would not show up and that this would be a fiasco for Ismail. I held my gaze, and he skulked away with his cronies. I will never forget the moment Nargis walked up on the stage and addressed the audience: She looked so beautiful as she spoke to us about the younger generation and its responsibility toward music, drama and art. Later in life, when I was making films, I again learned that there are times when people with bad intentions, for reasons of their own or just perversity, will try to trip you up, sliding like snakes across your path.

In my fourth and final year at St. Xavier's, I began to apply to American universities for admission to postgraduate business schools. I wrote to all the obvious places: Harvard, Yale, the University of Chicago, New York University and, of course, the University of Southern California, which was on the doorstep of Hollywood and, therefore, from my point of view, the ideal choice. New York University was the only one that offered me a place, and I was thrilled to receive the acceptance. Even though New York was a long way from Hollywood and I had never been there, it was a city I felt I knew intimately. This knowledge came from the movies, especially the Rock Hudson and Doris Day comedies that painted New York with a glamour and so-

phistication that made it seem like my kind of town. Every New York street was, according to the movies, paved with gold.

There was only one drawback: I didn't have the funds to pay the university fees. My father's resources were limited, and he could only provide a portion of the costs. My fellow students at St. Xavier's with whom I had worked to put on the college shows over the years now took it on themselves to organize a variety show with Shankar and Jaikishan as the guests of honor. They raised twenty thousand rupees—a fortune in those days—and, touchingly, gave that money to me as a gift toward my American studies. During our time at college we had combined our individual talents in art, music and theater to form an adventurous and very successful group that contributed to one of the strongest and most influential periods of St. Xavier's history. Later, when I began making films, I found myself repeating this process, bringing together talented individuals whom I would work with again and again over the years.

I left Bombay for New York on August 11, 1958, taking the boat from Bombay to Genoa, then the train to London, where I would spend a few days with my friend Karim before flying to New York.

Karim and I had grown up together virtually as brothers, our families being very close. He was a year ahead of me at St. Xavier's College, and was already a year into his law studies in London. He came to meet me at London's Victoria Station, where I felt a little chilly in spite of the August day. We took a taxi to his lodgings in Hampstead, and he introduced me to his landlady, a frosty, unwelcoming woman. "How," I asked Karim, "do you keep warm here?" Karim showed me a small gas fire, which also heated the water for a bath, that came to life only if you fed coins into a nearby slot meter. This seemed a very expensive way to keep warm and clean. Not that I really minded. I was in London. The London of *Brief Encounter*, and early Hitchcock movies where the city always seemed to be shrouded in fog. It was also the London of history books and literature: Queen Victoria, Disraeli, Shake-

With Karim at a Thursday-night dance at a frequent haunt of ours, the Radio Club, in Bombay.

speare, Wordsworth. Suddenly all the names I had grown up with had a context: Buckingham Palace, the Houses of Parliament, Big Ben and Westminster Bridge all lay before me, solid and inviting.

There was Trafalgar Square, and Speaker's Corner at Marble Arch on the edge of Hyde Park, where every Sunday people gave fiery speeches on topics I could scarcely fathom. Most of them were about the unjust lot of the working man who was exploited and brutalized by big business. And there was Leicester Square, and Shaftesbury Avenue with the cinemas and theaters, and the wonderfully seedy atmosphere of the drinking dens and clip joints of Soho, where decades later I would have an office. Hampstead, too, with its green spaces and arty atmosphere had its attractions—I loved wandering around the winding streets looking into the shops, and having lunch in one of the old-fashioned wood-paneled pubs, or just sitting by the pond and feeding the ducks and pigeons.

There was a moment when I seriously considered staying in London: I liked the place; Karim was there, and through him I had met other people. The prospect of going to New York, where I would be on my own, suddenly seemed daunting. But, to coin a terrible cliché, New York was calling me. I knew my destiny lay there.

Disillusion set in within hours of my arrival in New York. My home was a dingy room on the sixteenth floor of the Martinique Hotel in Herald Square, an area whose streets were not so much paved with gold as with inebriate bums clutching their bottles of cheap liquor. The chances of bumping into Doris Day or Rock Hudson as I walked around the neighborhood suddenly seemed very remote. And I was unlikely to encounter them in the local Horn & Hardart, where I was introduced to the novel concept of coin-operated food. Everything seemed to work on the principle of the slot machine. I had been lured to New York by the make-believe world of the

HOLLF

BORN

DIED

IN HONOR OF
XANDER LYMAN
REMOST AMONG
SE GENIUS AND
BLISHED IN A
AND IMPROV
GHOUT THE

movies, and had been terribly let down. "What have I come to?" I asked my-self. "What kind of a place *is* this?" My dreams were shattered—so far re-moved was this experience from the celluloid promise.

The next day I took a taxi to the International House on Riverside Drive at 123rd Street, and as the driver negotiated the Upper East Side and Cen-tral Park, cutting through areas that seemed more inviting and interesting, things started looking up. The International House, which is run by the Rockefeller Foundation, was where a number of students who had traveled on the boat from Bombay were staying, and I thought I might be able to get a room there too. I put my name on the waiting list, and no sooner had I re-turned to the hotel than I got a call from International House telling me that a room had become temporarily available, so I packed my bags and bid good-bye to the Martinique.

I remember getting my first letter from home and then bursting into tears with homesickness. I felt like a gypsy, moving from one place to an-other, unsettled and still unfamiliar with my surroundings. And there was worse to come. When my time was up at International House, I found a room in an apartment on the Upper West Side. The landlady was German and so terrifying that I dreaded coming face-to-face with her, so I would peep through the keyhole of my room to make sure she wasn't around before sneaking into the kitchen or the bathroom. The other two lodgers, a con-struction worker and a disabled man in a wheelchair, were equally weird, and the whole scenario seemed to belong in a horror movie.

Meanwhile, because I had very little money, I had to find a job. I went to the Indian Consulate and finessed my way into the office of Mr. Ayer, the secretary of the Indian Mission, who needed some additional staff to take care of the delegates arriving from India to attend the annual General As-sembly. "Do you know New York?" he asked. "Oh, yes," I replied. "I know New York very well." The job paid ninety dollars a week, part-time. There was no other answer I could have given.

I went down to Washington Square to enroll at New York University. I loved the park, the architecture of the brownstones, the cobbled streets and,

above all, the young people who inhabited the area. I knew I could be happy there, and wanted to find a room or an apartment share in that neighborhood. I was so desperate to move out of the German stalag that when another temporary vacancy became available at International House, I jumped at it. I was delighted to discover a close friend from St. Xavier's there and, together with a friend of his, we decided to rent an apartment in Brooklyn Heights.

One of the first things I did was to visit the Empire State Building. I took the tour to the very top of what was then the tallest building in the world, and half expected to see King Kong swinging from the pinnacle. I was standing on the top of the world and, as I looked across New York, I knew this was the place to be, this was the place where one could prove oneself. It is impossible to look down from the Empire State Building at the view of that great city, radiating opportunity and promise, and not be filled with a sense of energy and optimism. No matter how bleak my life seemed at that moment, I knew the movies hadn't lied. New York was the greatest city in the world, even if, at ground level, things didn't look quite so rosy. The message from the top of the Empire State Building was clear: This is New York and anything is possible.

That certainly seemed to be the case when I began the work of guiding Indian delegates around a city of which I was entirely ignorant. I had claimed to know New York intimately, and I only came unstuck once. Some delegates asked me whether there were any interesting hot spots I could take them to. Well, the hottest spot in New York at that time, from a student's point of view at least, was the Coffee House on MacDougal Street in the Village, where Allen Ginsberg read his poetry to adoring admirers. Of course this was not the kind of hot spot the delegates had in mind, and they were very disappointed. They wanted go-go dancers and strippers, and my knowledge of such establishments was thin. I knew there were some rather shady places around Forty-second Street, so I took my delegates there and fetched up at a place where the girls all looked sensational—dead ringers for Marilyn Monroe and Jayne Mansfield. I felt very pleased with myself, but what I didn't know was that this was a transvestite bar and that the "girls" were, in fact, boys. The delegates were less than thrilled when they made the discovery.

As the messenger for the Indian delegates I had the privilege of access to the Delegates' Lounge, and it was there that I began to entertain the financiers who might bankroll my first film. For all my other activities, I never lost sight of that aim. I befriended the beautiful Brazilian receptionist whose job it was to announce the meetings with the delegates, and I persuaded her to announce me as the Indian delegate whenever I entertained potential investors at lunch there.

Around this time I went to see a performance of *Sweet Bird of Youth*, which was then running on Broadway with Paul Newman, an actor whose films I had seen and admired in Bombay. Afterwards I managed to get backstage to introduce myself to Mr. Newman by persuading the stage doorkeeper that I had come all the way from Bombay to meet him and that he was expecting me. Mr. Newman, however, was quite surprised to discover a young Indian stranger knocking at the door of his dressing room, but he graciously invited me in. I congratulated him on his performance and told him I had come from India to learn about making films and that perhaps we might work together someday in India. We chatted for a while, and then I left. Outside, as I was sheltering under an awning waiting for the rain to stop, I noticed Mr. Newman leaving the theater and waved to him. As he got on his motorbike, he called out to me. "Which way are you heading?" he asked. "Downtown," I replied. "I'm going that way too. Hop on." So I got a ride home on the back of Paul Newman's bike. Twenty-eight years later I invited him and Joanne Woodward to dinner to discuss making *Mr. and Mrs. Bridge*, in which they would star. The film was from a script by Ruth Prawer Jhabvala and was to be directed by Jim Ivory. Over dinner I recounted the tale of our first encounter, and Paul was very surprised and amused. "So *you* were that crazy Indian," he said. I nodded. Here was Paul Newman, my hero from the days of St. Xavier's, and now we were going to make a film together.

Gradually my social circle started to expand, and so did my familiarity with the customs and habits of New York. I had been given an introduction

to Ali Razak, an Indian gentleman from Hyderabad and a longtime resident in New York, and through him I met Joseph and Bernice O'Reilly, a charming couple who lived in the Village and soon became good friends of mine. They invited me and my roommates to dinner at least once a week, when Bernice would cook Irish stew and bake soda bread. After dinner Bernice would sing show tunes for us accompanied by Joseph on the piano: *Diamonds Are a Girl's Best Friend* was a particular favorite.

Through the O'Reillys I met Jane Mosley, a striking half-Cherokee, half-black girl who was involved in fashion and modeling. I had never heard of Harlem, and knew nothing of Creole food, Afro fashions, jazz music and the marvelous Apollo Theater—the whole vibrant subculture that existed then and was entirely new and exciting to me. Blacks and whites mingled freely in New York, but two entirely different worlds existed within a few miles of each other.

When plans for *Divali,* the festival of lights that marked the Hindu New Year, were being made at International House, I suggested to Jane that we should reproduce the human puppet routine that I had staged and performed for one of my shows at St. Xavier's: a routine that I had originally pinched from the film *Chori Chori,* which starred Raj Kapoor and Nargis. This sequence was so successful that we were asked to repeat it for the Metropolitan Channel on television, and that was enough to persuade me to tackle a short film. All I needed was money.

I consulted the Manhattan telephone directory and made a list of all the film production companies. Many of the executives took the bait of lunch in the Delegates' Lounge at the United Nations—where, of course, the accommodating Brazilian receptionist announced me as an Indian delegate—but nothing ever came of those meetings. However, I did raise the interest of Charles Schwep of Trident Films, who seemed genuinely intrigued by the possibility of a film with an Indian mythological theme.

No sooner had I perfected this unlikely role of an Indian diplomat trying to raise money for a film, than Mr. Ayer, who had employed me as a messenger, got to hear of my activities in the Delegates' Lounge and called me in to see him. "So," he said, "I understand you are posing as a delegate." "No, sir," I replied. "Not exactly. I was just trying to make some connections so that our delegates could make the best use of their time here." I think Mr. Ayer was rather amused by my chutzpah, so he didn't fire me.

In any case, my temporary job as guide was coming to an end after three months, so I went along to the Indian Tourist Centre to see if they had any vacancies. There was no work for me there, but I met the person in charge of public relations, a very refined, good-looking young gentleman who spoke flawless English and perfect Urdu. His name was Saeed Jaffrey, and he was no more a public relations expert than I was a tour guide. He was, in fact, an actor, and both he and his wife, Madhur Jaffrey, were studying at the Actors Studio with Lee Strasberg. We got along so well that he invited me to his home for dinner, where I met Madhur, a very attractive, regal-looking woman who was then expecting their first child. Madhur would eventually become an award-winning actress as well as the great authority on Indian cooking, but all that was still a long way away. The Jaffreys lived in what was once O. Henry's apartment on Twenty-sixth Street, to which I became a frequent visitor. I loved their company, the artistic milieu they moved in and the exquisite meals Saeed and Madhur prepared. I could not then have imagined that this would be the most important connection I would make in my life: Through Madhur and Saeed I eventually met James Ivory. But that, too, was still a long way away.

In the meantime, I continued looking for work and applied to the advertising agency McCann-Erickson, where I was interviewed by a gentleman named William Schneider, who seemed to think I had the makings of an account-executive trainee and offered me a job.

After three months in Brooklyn, my flatmates and I moved to an apartment at 33 Washington Square West, a building where Eleanor Roosevelt had once lived. I was a great admirer of Mrs. Roosevelt, and I can still remember how thrilled I was to see her at close quarters when she came to give an address at the United Nations and attended a reception in her honor afterwards.

Our new apartment overlooked the Waverly Cinema, and was a stone's throw from the Eighth Street Playhouse, the Fifth Avenue Cinema and Cinema Village. I was like a child let loose in a candy store as I went from one cinema to another. It was in those theaters that I discovered European films and the work of Truffaut, Fellini, De Sica and Bergman. And it was there that I first saw the films of Satyajit Ray, whose work I had heard about in India but, because his films were rarely shown outside West Bengal, had never had an opportunity to see. Those films were inspiring: They were the kind I wanted to make.

As for my studies, well, in keeping with the pattern I had established in Bombay, I neglected my academic work to the point where I rarely managed to achieve anything better than a B grade for my papers. The problem this time was not the distraction of my other activities, but simply that I did not like the classes. While some of these classes were held at the main body of the university in Washington Square, most took place at a business school on Wall Street, where they attracted many business executives seeking advancement, so there was none of the atmosphere of student camaraderie that one expects from university life. I was surprised by the informality of the tutorials and the easygoing attitude of students who sat through the lectures with their feet up on the desks. I can remember thinking that Americans had enormous feet—and was appalled that the professors didn't seem to mind conducting their lectures in this fashion.

In those years, Wall Street was a ghost town in the evenings, when most of my classes took place—presumably to accommodate the working hours of the "mature" students—so there was little inducement to leave the funkier atmosphere of Greenwich Village. I was very conscious of the expense of this degree, however, and made an effort to improve my grades. I had also become very fond of two of my tutors, Jake Corbin and John Lennard, and I didn't want to disappoint them. So I began to study hard. At the end of eighteen months I graduated.

When my job at the United Nations came to an end, so too did access to the Delegates' Lounge, and I now had nowhere to entertain potential in-

vestors. I could hardly invite them to dine at Chock full o' Nuts, which was all I could afford. It was around this time that I began cooking with the goal of entertaining people at home. However, coming from a very traditional Indian background, where men never ventured into the kitchen, I knew little about how to prepare food. Like most middle-class families, we had a cook at home, and the preparation of every meal was supervised by my mother, who was an excellent cook herself.

The only experience I ever had with cooking was at a school picnic while I was at high school in Bombay, and even then my role was that of delegator rather than chef. The class was often taken on field trips, and on one occasion I suggested that instead of eating at a restaurant as we usually did, we should prepare our own meal, rather like a picnic. Because this had been my idea, I became the organizer, sending boys off to the market to buy meat and vegetables and rice, and other boys to borrow a cauldron and pots from a restaurant. Others had to find wood and make a fire, or collect banana leaves that we used as plates. It was rather like being a film producer: assigning people to various tasks and coordinating the whole affair. When all the food was bubbling away in the pots, I would go from one to the other giving a stir, or adding some spice, until the food was ready to be dished up. The professor who had accompanied the class was very much impressed with the result—for which I took all the credit.

But in New York I didn't have forty classmates to help me, though, by an odd coincidence, the first victims of my cooking included a professor, John Lennard, my tutor at the university, and his wife, Martha, together with the Jaffreys. I had the good sense not to attempt anything too ambitious—a simple *keema*—a kind of spiced mincemeat stew with peas, rice and dal—and a salad. The result was a great success, and so cooking became a useful tool when I entertained financiers, bankers, actors and all the other people essential to making a film. Producers usually wine and dine such people at the finest—and most expensive—restaurants. This producer cooked for them, and I'm sure the novelty of the arrangement played a part in motivating some to agree to my schemes for getting films done.

As a child I was always in the kitchen agitating and complaining because the cook was taking too long to prepare the meal, but even though I was hungry and impatient, I must have absorbed a great deal about the techniques of cooking without being aware of it. Either that or I was an instinctive cook, for I was never taught how to do it, nor did I follow recipes. But I gradually discovered that I was able to recreate the flavors I had grown up with.

I was working at McCann-Erickson when Charles Schwep, one of the people I had lured to lunch at the Delegates' Lounge, put up nine thousand dollars for my first film, *The Creation of Woman,* a fourteen-minute short based on the Indian mythological story of the Hindu god Brahma. I had intended to perform in this with Madhur Jaffrey, but this was largely a dance-and-mime piece, and Schwep, who was directing the film, felt it would be better served by professional dancers. We approached Bhaskar Roy Chaudhuri, a celebrated Indian dancer in New York, to play the lead. I don't think Schwep believed Bhasker would agree to take part in such a small project, but I felt we had nothing to lose by asking. So I asked, and Chaudhuri agreed to perform, alongside two of his students, Dino and Rani. Jim McIntyre, an art director at McCann-Erickson, designed the set.

We shot the film over three nights in a studio on the West Side, and every morning after we'd wrapped, we would go to the Horn & Hardart on West Fifty-seventh Street, where you could get a huge breakfast for a dollar and a half. I was now a film producer, so I decided to go to Hollywood.

Just before leaving New York, I asked my friend Patrick Hanegan, who worked as the press agent for Canadian Railways, to prepare a press release for all the Los Angeles and the New York papers announcing my arrival in Los Angeles. A REAL HEP VISITOR FROM INDIA blazed the headline above the story in the *New York Herald Tribune:*

> Ismail Merchant of Bombay, descendant of an ancient Indian Mogul family, will shortly depart from New York for Hollywood . . . more surprising that Mr. Merchant is what we Americans greatly admire, and possibly do not expect an Indian to be: a cracker-barrel fireball,

whose personality and ability "epitomize all that is purposeful, vigorous and energetic in the new India," according to some press material about him. . . .

This caught the attention of Pat Weaver, who was then the chairman of McCann-Erickson's international division, and he asked to see me, curious to know about this jumped-up employee who was getting all the publicity. "Clearly you are a very bright person," he said, judging that this kind of self-promotion boded well for a career in advertising. "We shall have to keep an eye on you."

Many years later I was to meet Mr. Weaver again, in the company of his daughter Sigourney, whom we were trying to cast in our film *The Bostonians*. I invited them to dinner, and listened as he amused Sigourney with the story of how we had met. "I always knew you would work miracles," he said to me.

I took the train to Los Angeles, and as I got nearer and nearer to Nirvana, I prepared for the press avalanche that would greet me at the railway station. The press release would surely generate nothing less than a red carpet and the flashing bulbs of dozens of newspaper photographers eager to record this historic arrival of the great Indian film producer. The welcome was rather more muted than the one I had imagined. There was no red carpet, no photographers, no studio executives clutching contracts for me—even the person who was supposed to meet me failed to show up.

Bernice O'Reilly had arranged for me to stay with friends of hers, Yvonne and Carlos Rodriguez, who lived in Culver City, right by MGM's back lot. My dream was tantalizingly close, only a wall separated us, but it was a well-protected wall that was more difficult to penetrate than I had anticipated. In the scenario I had mapped out in my mind, I would show my film to studio executives who would immediately recognize a brilliant new talent and offer me the chance to make movies. If that failed, I would switch to Plan B, which involved becoming a star in Hollywood films, rather as Sabu had done. The possibility that either of these schemes would fail to materialize never crossed my mind.

Interestingly, even at that stage my goal was to introduce audiences to the culture of India. There had been some attempts—notably Renoir's brilliant film *The River* and, on a more mundane level, films like *Bhowani Junction*—but I felt that there was a great deal of rich material that had never been properly explored by filmmakers, and I was the person to do it. I was, as usual, ahead of my time, and the public's fascination with Indian culture and mysticism was still many years away.

Telephone calls to the studios to inquire about work yielded little hope: There was no demand for an Indian film producer. So I got a part-time job at a clothing store in Westwood and became a very successful salesman. The salary was small, but I earned a commission on everything I sold: When a man came into the store to buy a suit, I sold him four. My boss offered me a permanent job, and even proposed a partnership. "No, no," I said, "I am going to make movies." In the meantime, I took a second job working until four o'clock in the morning on the night shift in the classified ads department of the *Los Angeles Times*, and moved from Culver City to a room in downtown L.A.

I considered taking a film course at the University of Southern California, but I knew I was not temperamentally suited to academic life. Instead, I approached the film department at the university and offered my services as a visiting Indian producer. I suggested they might, perhaps, like me to give a talk to the students on Indian cinema, illustrated with a screening of the popular Hindi film *Barsaat*, starring Nimmi and directed by Raj Kapoor, a copy of which I managed to find in Los Angeles. They responded with great enthusiasm to the idea.

I visited the studios and through their public relations departments found my way onto sound stages where I established more and more contacts, introducing myself as an Indian producer looking to cast Hollywood stars in films I was planning to make in India. This was not exactly the truth, but I didn't perceive it as a lie: I was confident that I would eventually do all the things I was setting out to do. I was just a little ahead of myself.

I met Agnes Moorehead when she was shooting at Universal Studios. One of Orson Welles's Mercury Theatre players, Agnes Moorehead was an actress I had admired since seeing her in *The Magnificent Ambersons*. We took to each other immediately, and she later hosted a small dinner for me at her grand house on North Roxbury Drive in Beverly Hills, for which I prepared an Indian meal. After dinner she screened *The Creation of Woman*. Among her guests that night were representatives from a number of Hollywood studios, including Blair Berman from the Fox Cinema circuit.

When I tried to register *The Creation of Woman* for an Academy Award nomination, I was told that the film was ineligible because it had not played the statutory three days in a commercial theater during the year. As the year was now coming to an end, there seemed little chance the film could qualify. But I was not prepared to hang around for another twelve months, so I went to see Blair Berman, Agnes Moorehead's friend at Fox, and suggested to him that my film could play alongside Bergman's *The Devil's Eye*, which was then being shown at the Fine Arts Cinema, part of the Fox circuit. He agreed to this and screened my film for a week, making it eligible for a nomination, a nomination it was unlikely to get unless a significant number of Academy members saw it—and I made sure they did. I also invited Philip Scher, the film critic of the *Los Angeles Times*, who gave it a glowing review.

I returned to the Academy to register my film. "I told you to come back next year," barked the lady who had sent me away the first time. I told her my film had now played in Los Angeles, but she didn't believe me. I showed her the review, but she didn't believe that either and went off to get her own copy of the paper, obviously suspicious that I had had a page fraudulently printed. "Very well," she said, having compared her copy of the paper with mine. "Fill in the application form," which I did. The film was then screened for Academy members, and attracted enough votes to be nominated in the live-action short film category. Allied Artists then offered to distribute the film worldwide. In those days, short films had a good chance of playing with feature films, but that practice has now disappeared. Short films are rarely shown in cinemas today, only on television. I was lucky that *Creation of Woman* opened so many doors for me.

The idea for my first feature film had been brewing for some time. It was

I met with Aldous Huxley in Los Angeles in 1960. We shared an interest in Indian mythology, and I showed Huxley my film Creation of Woman.

to be an almost autobiographical, but fictionalized, story of an Indian coming to Hollywood to make movies. All I needed was a writer—and money. I approached Isobel Lennart, a highly regarded screenwriter at MGM, who was sympathetic to the idea of writing something for me. During our conversation she mentioned that she had just read a wonderful book called *The Householder* by Ruth Prawer Jhabvala, which she suggested I should consider filming. "Hollywood would never make it," I remember her saying, "but you should." Even then, Ruth had admirers among Hollywood's literary community.

I bought a copy of the book and read it, and then made a note in my diary that it would be my first film in India. At that time I was toying with another idea for a film set in Los Angeles and India called *Destiny of Life,* for which I had neither script nor financing, but I did have two stars—Agnes Moorehead and Ernest Castaldo. The film was never made, although we did shoot some footage of the *mahurat* ceremony of priests chanting traditional hymns to bring luck. This footage, filmed in a beautiful house in the Hollywood Hills, emerged in a later film, *Bombay Talkie*.

After a year in Los Angeles I returned to New York en route to the Cannes Film Festival, where *The Creation of Woman* had been accepted in competition. Ernest Castaldo, who had just completed filming *West Side Story*, was also going to New York, so we decided to drive back together, stopping briefly in Washington, where I had arranged to meet the Indian ambassador, M. C. Chagla, and tell him about my plans to make films in India for Western audiences. Ambassador Chagla came from a very distinguished family and was the most famous barrister in India, as well as a close supporter of the Congress Party, which dominated Indian politics for decades. His sister, Nuru Swaminathan, an alumna of St. Xavier's, was later of great assistance to us during the making of *The Guru*, helping us to recruit teenagers for the pop star scenes in that film.

We arrived in New York late at night, and Ernest had arranged for me to spend the night with a friend of his. I left all my belongings—clothes, documents, press cuttings—in the car. The next morning we discovered the car had been broken into and everything had been taken. It was a terrible blow, but one has to be philosophical about such things.

I contacted Madhur and Saeed to tell them about the success of *The Creation of Woman* and that I was on my way to Cannes. Saeed, who had narrated my film, told me that I should see *The Sword and the Flute*, a documentary on Indian miniature painting made by a very special American from Oregon named James Ivory, so he invited me to a screening at India House. Saeed had also narrated Jim's film, and although he had previously mentioned the name to me, I had never met him.

The subject of Indian miniature painting was one that I knew very little about, and I found the film completely absorbing and moving. The idea of using the history of this medium to explore historical events, life and spirituality was both original and complex, and Jim's intelligent script and striking choice of music by Ravi Shankar and Ali Akbar Khan made this a very compelling work.

After the screening we were introduced, and I invited him for coffee. I was intrigued that a thirty-three-year-old from Oregon knew so much about India, and I was interested to know more about this American who had such an empathy with the culture of my country. We went to a coffeehouse called the Right Bank on Madison Avenue at Sixty-sixth Street. On this point we both agree, but from here on our accounts of what happened next diverge considerably.

I remember listening attentively to Jim, an attractive, aquiline-featured man, as he talked about his film. He is a quiet, unassuming person, and he needed gentle prodding to volunteer information about himself and his work. *The Sword and the Flute* was his second film, after *Venice: Theme and Variations*, which had followed a similar pattern, examining Venice through the eyes of painters from Canaletto to Saul Steinberg. He knew more about Indian music, art and films than most Indians. And we found we had similar tastes and many points of common interest—especially in the films of Satyajit Ray, whose work we both admired and whom Jim had had the privilege of meeting in India. Those are my memories of that evening.

Jim, on the other hand, insists that as soon as we arrived at the coffeehouse, I left him and went to make phone calls, and then spent the whole evening running between our table and the phone booth to call financiers and other important people. At one point, according to Jim, I even borrowed a dime from him because I had run out of change for the phone. I don't think so, especially because I was trying to entice Jim, who was keen to return to India to finish a film about Delhi commissioned by the Asia Society, to come to India and work with me. We will probably never resolve this, but what is beyond dispute is that Merchant Ivory Productions was born on that late April night in 1961 with the intention of making Indian-themed films for an international audience. A plaque on the wall of the Right Bank will mark the historic occasion.

I arranged a screening of *The Creation of Woman* for Jim, after which he invited me to dinner at his apartment on Sixty-second Street at Lexington Avenue. Among his extensive record collection was the music of Nazakat and

Salamat Ali Khan, two brilliant Pakistani vocal musicians whom I had seen perform years earlier at the R K Studios in Bombay when I accompanied Nimmi to a concert. It was the first time I had heard their music since I had been in America. Jim enjoyed vocal Indian classical music as much as I did: Like opera, you need to have a special feeling to appreciate this particular music. This more than anything else, I think, cemented our friendship. We spent many hours in his apartment sitting on the little balcony, discussing the work of Ray and other directors we admired. I still have many of the black-and-white photographs he took of me at that time—striking portraits that reveal an artist's skill in capturing the essence of his subject.

Jim never set out to be a director. He had studied architecture and fine arts at the University of Oregon with the idea of becoming a set designer, and then took a postgraduate course in filmmaking at the University of Southern California. In his strong visual sense and gift for composition he seemed to have the makings of an outstanding cinematographer, and that is

James Ivory directing me in The Guru, *one of our earliest collaborations.*

probably the path he would have followed. The director Sidney Meyers had asked Jim to photograph *Devgar*, a film he was planning to make in India from a script by Gitel Steed, a kind of anthropological study of a Gujarati village, for which he was then trying to raise money. I offered to help them find funding in India.

Soon after this I left for the Cannes Film Festival. When I arrived, I discovered that my film had been rescheduled: I had missed its screening on the previous evening. I was very disappointed, even though Gene Moskowitz, the chief film critic of *Variety*, had seen the film and given it a very good review in his paper. I also learned that my accreditation as a participant in the festival had not been completed, so I was unable to attend any of the screenings or events, which eliminated any chance I had of connecting with the investors and film financiers I had set my sights on.

But even though my visit to Cannes hadn't worked out in the way I had hoped, I was in high spirits when I left France: I was returning home to India for the first time in three years, I would see my family again and I was about to make my first feature film.

My family, eagerly looking forward to my return, had no idea of the nightmare that was about to be visited on them. No sooner had I arrived in Bombay than I decided that we should sell the apartment at Nul Bazaar and move the whole family to a larger place. We found a suitable apartment in a smarter neighborhood, but the new apartment seemed to demand new furniture, so all the old furniture was sold.

I was trying to raise money and find a cast for *Devgar* when Betty Delgarno, an Australian working for an advertising agency, called me out of the blue to invite me to a party. Betty offered her help with casting *Devgar*, as well as any other general assistance she could give to the production, and mentioned that she knew a rather dashing young actor, Shashi Kapoor. I had heard of Shashi, of course; he was part of a major theatrical dynasty. His father was Prithviraj Kapoor, the legendary actor, director and producer

of both theater and film, and Shashi's brothers, Raj Kapoor and Shammi Kapoor, were also actors. But I had never seen Shashi perform; he had made only one film at that point and, although it had not yet been released, his performance and screen presence had already created a loud buzz.

Betty took me to meet Shashi, and I shall never forget the impact he made on me when he opened the door of his apartment. He was tall, very handsome, hugely charismatic and had *star* written all over him. I saw no reason to waste time.

James Ivory and his young star of The Householder, *Shashi Kapoor.*

"I am Ismail Merchant," I said. "I am here from America to make films, and you will star in them." Shashi was entertaining a bunch of rather drunk journalists that night, and he probably thought I was not entirely sober either. He seemed rather taken aback by my approach, but by the end of the evening I had infected him with my enthusiasm, and he became very interested in *Devgar.*

As all the elements began to come together, we needed a space in which to organize the operation, so I found a tiny one-room office in Bombay's financial district. There was just enough space for a desk—and not too many people. We also needed a lawyer to handle the contracts and legal work, and Taher Doctor, a fellow student from St. Xavier's who was now a partner in a legal practice, volunteered to represent us. When Jim arrived in India in November, we went along to the High Court in Bombay to file our partnership registration papers. We were now officially a company—Merchant Ivory Productions—and the company was incorporated in New York the following year.

Devgar was abandoned, however, because it was impossible to interest financiers in such an esoteric project. So I asked Jim to read *The Householder*, and he was very taken by Ruth's delightful comedy, set in Delhi, about a newly married couple and their interfering mother-in-law.

Obviously, it was meant to happen this way. I had never heard of Ruth Prawer Jhabvala, a German author married to an Indian and living in Delhi, and would probably never have read the book had it not been recommended to me by Isobel Lennart in Hollywood. There were strange forces at work here—inescapable destiny. Ruth Prawer Jhabvala, however, did not want to share this destiny. When I telephoned her from Bombay to introduce myself, she pretended to be her mother-in-law in order to get rid of me. By nature a rather self-contained person who values her solitude, Ruth does not welcome the intrusion of strangers into her life. She had been approached by BBC producers in the past, and because nothing had ever come of those advances, she regarded film people as time wasters and, quite possibly, charlatans. This didn't stop Jim and me from going to Delhi, armed with my huge portfolio of press clippings, to try to impress her. Jim had met Ruth on a previous visit to Delhi at a Christmas party, at which, according to Jim, after just two drinks Ruth had gone to lie down. Ruth has always denied this, but it probably explains why she had only the haziest memory of ever having met Jim.

When we called Ruth from Delhi, she agreed, out of a sense of politeness, to meet us for tea at her home, a beautiful house designed by her husband, Cyrus Jhabvala, a successful architect. I showed her my portfolio: the HEP VISITOR FROM INDIA headlines; photographs of me with Agnes Moorehead, Lucille Ball and other Hollywood stars; the reviews of my film; the press releases—all of which she looked at impassively. If I'd hoped to impress her, I'd fallen wide of the mark. Jim, however, quieter and less excitable, seemed to connect with her, and she finally agreed to let us have the rights to *The Householder*. Jim suggested that Ruth should write the screenplay, but she told us that she had never written a screenplay. That was not a problem. I had never produced a feature film, and Jim had never directed one. To our astonishment, she produced the screenplay in something like ten days.

Ruth may have suspected that nothing would come of this association, but her husband Jhab was certain that we were fly-by-night rogues. He warned Ruth not to get involved with us—that we would bring no joy to her life. In the forty years we have known each other he still claims, affectionately, that I have given him no reason to revise that opinion.

Jim wrote to Satyajit Ray asking if we could use the services of his cinematographer, Subrata Mitra, to shoot our film. Ray recommended us to Mitra, who agreed to the proposal and brought with him his usual team from Calcutta. Mitra seemed a very grand man, but his intense, serious expression disguised a great sense of humor. Strong willed and demanding about his work, he was a great artist who wrought visual miracles because of his uncompromising attitude to the framing and composition of scenes. Always dressed in elegant Indian clothes, usually of white homespun *khadi*, and a habitual chain-smoker, he cut an authoritative figure on set. His stern appearance was deceptive, though: He enjoyed the pleasures of life, particularly good food—for which he would roll up his sleeves and dig in.

Looking back on that time, I am struck at how inexorable the process of making *The Householder* was. It seems as if one minute I was on Jim's terrace in New York discussing plans and schemes in totally abstract terms, and the next we were in Delhi ready to shoot the film. I will certainly never forget the look of panic in Jim's eyes when we went to the train station in Delhi to meet the technicians who had come from Calcutta to work on the film. He looked at the mountain of equipment they had brought with them—the camera, the lights, the cables and all the other paraphernalia of filmmaking—and the reality of the situation finally hit him. He suggested we call the whole thing off.

Jim wasn't the only one with second thoughts. Ruth's worst fears about filmmakers were confirmed when she met Shashi. The character Ruth had created in her novel was an unremarkable schoolteacher, and to have that part played by this very glamorous man made her heart sink. Worse, the role of his wife in the film was being played by Leela Naidu, a beautiful French-Indian actress I had met in Bombay at a party given by Betty Delgarno.

These were not the ordinary people of Ruth's imagination, and she accepted our decision with reservations.

In March we began filming *The Householder* in Delhi, where I had found our principal location by chance rather than design. On my way to meet Jim when he arrived in Delhi from the United States, a fellow passenger on the train was Ustad Zafar Khan, a distinguished sitar player who had appeared at the concerts I had organized at St. Xavier's. He was staying with friends who lived in Daryaganj and invited me to visit him there, unaware of the chain of events this casual invitation would set in motion.

Both the area and the home of Zafar Khan's friend, Inder Narayan, seemed to correspond precisely with the descriptions Ruth had given in her book. I climbed the narrow stairs of a modest house and emerged on a rooftop terrace. There, opposite, set closely against the pale dusty-pink evening sky of winter were three black-and-white-striped, melon-shaped domes of a small Moghul mosque, and the requisite pair of minarets. Sounds of the city floated up, and small lights twinkled everywhere. It seemed to me

Indu (Leela Naidu) and Prem (Shashi Kapoor) on the roof of their house over-looking the Zeenat mosque.

at once to be the perfect location for the one-room flat of the young couple, Prem and Indu, in *The Householder*. It had just one biggish room and a stupendous view. The mosque—called the Zeenat Mosque and built by Zeenat Begum, a daughter of the Emperor Aurangzeb, in the late seventeenth century—was of white marble, rather austerely decorated in line with her father's philosophy about art, which was, Less is more in all things (except warfare). Later, while shooting, we struggled somewhat when it came to fitting actors, equipment, furniture and crew into that room, but we managed somehow. Our cameraman Subrata Mitra was willing to put up with the inconvenience of our cramped quarters because of the compensating view, which was nearly always present in all kinds of weather and light, and most of the young couple's life was lived outdoors on their terrace.

Finding such an ideal location added, I believe, another dimension to the film: It not only gave the scenes a visual richness, but it also felt authentic, as if the characters really belonged there. Appropriate locations have since become one of the distinguishing features of our films, and through a combination of charm, guile and stubbornness, I have managed to gain access to places no filmmaker has ever been allowed to shoot before—King's College, Cambridge, for example, and the roof of the Palace at Versailles.

With everything finally in place we began shooting the first Merchant Ivory film. All those years of sitting in the college canteen drafting cast lists and dreaming of Hollywood had led to this moment. Sure, I didn't have Hedy Lamarr or Tyrone Power and Nimmi in my film, and I wasn't making it for a big Hollywood studio, but this was a step in the right direction.

The reality of making a feature film hit me like a thermonuclear device. Even on a small scale, a production like this requires absolute precision to avoid catastrophe. People, logistics and schedules need to be taken into account and coordinated. And I had failed to anticipate the amount of bureaucracy and red tape involved: the permissions that had to be applied for, the various ministries that had to be kept informed of our movements, the sheer frustration with the never-ending paperwork. And because there was no margin in our budget for someone to deal with all this, I ended up doing it

myself. When I wasn't at the typewriter composing letters, I functioned as the production manager, location manager, accountant, caterer and even chauffeur, driving the actors between their hotels and the location in my car. More than forty years and forty films later, I still take on those roles when the need arises.

But back then I simply hadn't allowed for it in my preparations: I was a novice. In the matter of press relations, however, I was a seasoned pro. There was no point in doing something unless the world knew about it, and I invited every journalist in the country to come and write about this momentous Indo-American collaboration. We even had a visit from Pearl Buck, who was about to do a film in India of R. K. Narayan's *The Guide*.

Jim's father had put up most of the money for the film; my father had also contributed some funds; and Shashi, who was getting paid practically nothing anyway, agreed to defer his entire fee. And then, halfway through shooting, the money ran out. This, and an intense heat wave in Delhi, compelled us to stop work. We had been shooting two versions of the film—in English and in Hindi—and, in retrospect, I think we were just too ambitious.

We sent the crew back to Calcutta, and returned to Bombay with the half-completed film, which Jim began to edit. Of course I was disappointed by this development, but when I saw the rushes of the footage, I was so absolutely certain this would be a successful film that I was fired up with enthusiasm to complete it. I approached every possible source of finance in India, including India's Film Financing Corporation, but everyone turned us down. The only films that were financed at that time were the all-singing, all-dancing marathon epics that embraced every implausible fantasy known to celluloid. Our intimate chamber piece didn't stand a chance. In desperation I turned to moneylenders, but their usurious terms would have made the Mafia blush.

Finally, I went to Mohamed Mitha, a family friend and owner of the Rex cinema in Bombay, who had already invested a small amount of money in the film with a view to showing it at his cinema. In the meantime, he had made a huge profit from *The Guns of Navarone*, a Columbia picture that had

been a worldwide success, and he agreed to increase his investment. We asked Jim's father and my father for more money, and together with loans from a couple of ex-college friends of mine, we were able to return to Delhi in August and finish the film. All told, it had cost $125,000. Mohamed Mitha, who had a vested interest in the film's success, offered to show some of the rushes to a visiting executive from Columbia Pictures who liked what he saw and suggested we take the finished film to New York to show to his colleagues.

Many years later I met Gregory Peck at a screening he was hosting of *The Golden Bowl* in Los Angeles. He had starred in *The Guns of Navarone*, and the success of that film was indirectly responsible for the completion of *The Householder*. When I addressed the audience, welcoming the guests to the screening, I told them that had it not been for Gregory Peck and the success of *The Guns of Navarone* in Bombay, we might never have finished our first film, which paved the road to success. I remember he had tears in his eyes as I told the story, and after the screening he told me that his only regret was that he had not appeared in *The Golden Bowl*.

I never cooked while we were filming—I had more than enough to occupy me—but I engaged a cook at the house where we were staying during the shooting, and each morning I would tell him what to prepare for the evening, what he had to buy and where to buy it. Because so many of our technicians came from Calcutta, and Bengalis love fish, I would often order that. And there would always be rice and vegetables, prepared in a variety of ways, plus *chappatis* and *parathas*. At lunchtime I would go to Moti Mahal, an excellent Punjabi restaurant, and order their specialities for the whole unit. Sometimes we would go there in the evening after shooting and listen to the musicians perform *quawali*. At other times we would go to the Chinese restaurant at the Ashoka Hotel, where Shashi was staying. But my favorite place was the kebab seller near the Jamma Masjid (the Moghul mosque) near the Red Fort, who made the most delicious kebabs. Every Friday I would go to prayers at the Jamma Masjid and come back loaded with kebabs and *roti* for the unit.

Shashi loved food—and wine. There was nothing he enjoyed more than socializing with friends over a table full of good food and lots of wine. Even after three years in America I had never drunk wine, and Shashi decided that it was time I was introduced to the better things in life. "If you have never tasted wine, then you have wasted your life," Shashi told me. "You must have one glass with me." He corrupted me completely.

After editing the film in Bombay, Jim wanted to show it to Satyajit Ray, both for his opinion and his advice, so we took the completed film to Ray in Calcutta. He told us he liked the film but felt it could be improved by tightening its structure. And then, in a typically generous Ray gesture, he offered to reshape the film for us. He asked to be given a free hand, but said that if we didn't like what he had done, he would put it back as it was. There was little chance of that. In just three days Ray and his editor, Dulal Dutta, a tiny, wiry man who knew his craft extremely well, worked on the film, giving it a flashback framework that vastly improved our own cut. In addition, he composed some of the music and supervised the recording. All of this was done by Ray in a spirit of generosity and friendship.

I will never forget my first encounter with Ray, at his apartment in Calcutta. Even if you knew nothing about him, you knew at once that you were in the presence of a grand man. In his living room there was an upright piano, paintings, photographs and books—thousands and thousands of books, on art, on music, on film; books on composers and writers and philosophers; and books of English and Bengali literature. At over six feet tall, with a chiseled face and a solemn manner, he was a very imposing figure. Normally I blabber away in my usual extroverted, excitable way, but in the presence of Ray I was struck dumb with awe. It must have taken Ray by surprise because I know that he had heard about me from various sources, particularly Subrata Mitra and other technicians who had worked with us, and I suspect he had been expecting a completely different Ismail from the one sitting quietly in his drawing room.

Jim had met Ray on an earlier visit to Calcutta when he was in India making *The Delhi Way*. He had looked Ray up in the telephone directory and,

with no prior introduction, simply called him up because he wanted to meet him. Ray, who had just finished *The Music Room*, a film he thought might be too specialized for a Western audience, offered to show it to Jim to get his opinion. Jim was thrilled with the film and expressed his immense enthusiasm to Ray.

Ray was always accessible; his door was open to anyone who needed anything, or just wanted to shake his hand. There were no gorillas to guard his privacy. He was humble and unassuming, and I'm sure he was completely unaware of the esteem in which he was held by so many people. As time passed, I became more relaxed in his presence, and we struck up a special friendship.

The first screening of *The Householder* was at the residence of John Ken-

At the party after the gala premiere of The House- holder, *held at the New Delhi residence of American Ambassador John Kenneth Galbraith (far left), with Billie Nuruddin. Seated, Prime Minister Nehru is flanked by Ruth Jhabvala (to his left) and me (to his right).*

neth Galbraith, the American ambassador, in New Delhi. Because the film was the first Indo-American coproduction, it seemed appropriate to have it premiered at Roosevelt House. This had been arranged through Mrs. Billie Nuruddin, the wife of the mayor of Delhi and a close friend of Ruth's. Among the many distinguished guests who attended were the prime minister of India, Jawaharlal Nehru, and his daughter (and future prime minister), Indira Gandhi, along with her two sons, Sanjay and Rajiv Gandhi.

All the film needed now was a distributor, but the odds of attracting any of the major players to such a small-scale film were slim without some international exposure. We thought the Venice Film Festival was the place for us, and submitted our film. At the same time, Jim's father decided to visit Venice and took the opportunity to meet me, the partner of his son, about whom he knew nothing except what he'd heard from Jim. I knew Ivory senior felt I was some kind of oriental adventurer, so when we met at the Gritti Palace Hotel,

From left to right, the director (James Ivory), stars (Leela Naidu, Shashi Kapoor) and producer (me) of The Householder, *Merchant Ivory Productions' first feature-length film, 1964.*

I think he was reassured to find a solid person with feet firmly planted on the ground.

Venice didn't want our film, and neither did the British distributors to whom I showed it in London. I remembered the Columbia Pictures executive who had expressed an interest in the film in Bombay, so although it seemed like a long shot, Jim and I took the SS *France* back to New York and showed our film to Columbia. They liked it very much, and we struck a worldwide distribution deal. One executive said the story could just as easily have been set in a Jewish community in the Bronx, and everyone could identify with the characters. When I had been trying to raise money for the film, the argument I kept coming up against was that such an "Indian" story would not have general appeal. But what could be more universal than a pair of newlyweds and an interfering mother-in-law?

What a victory that was! A film that Hollywood would never have made was now being distributed all over the world by a major Hollywood studio. It was the most wonderful feeling, but short-lived. Columbia took on the film, but they refused to pay us because of a tricky clause in the contract that necessitated the Indian government approving the transaction. The Indian government refused because they feared the film's success in India would add to the liability of repatriating rupees into hard currency. (The Indian government had limited foreign companies from changing money they made in India to their own currencies. The embargo did solve the problem.)

I immediately returned to Delhi and, with Jhab's help, began a battle with the bureaucrats. But it wasn't until the joint secretary in India threatened a total embargo on all American films that the matter was resolved. At that point I hurried to the Reserve Bank of India to deal with more bureaucrats who could unblock the rupees that were sitting in Columbia's account. After many months the money was finally paid to us per the agreement.

The Householder opened at the Guild Theater in New York in October 1963 to very good reviews from the critics in general. However, the *New York Times*—whose review mattered most—was unfavorable, and without a positive response from that paper, *The Householder* stood very little chance at the box office.

But we had made a film. Jim could now call himself a director, I could call myself a feature film producer and Ruth was indeed a screenwriter.

Jim had given me a copy of the diary of Lady Sale, a formidable English memsahib captured by the Afghans in 1854 when the British had to retreat from Kabul. It was a fascinating story, and we felt Vivien Leigh could be very good in the lead. I had invited Miss Leigh to an early screening of *The House-holder* at Columbia Pictures on Fifth Avenue through her very helpful agent, Kay Brown. She arrived and sat between Jim and me—imagine Scarlett O'Hara and Blanche Dubois sitting with us watching our first film. Some weeks later we had dinner together at a rooftop restaurant at 666 Fifth Avenue, and I told her about the film we had in mind. Vivien Leigh was born in India. She had a special connection to that part of the world, so she was very enthusiastic about the project and keen to do the film.

A couple of years later she came to India to visit some friends, and in interviews with the Delhi papers she spoke very highly of *The Householder* and said that she was looking forward to working with us. She arrived in Bombay and I went to greet her with a traditional flower garland, and made plans to take her to the Elephanta Caves.

Elephanta Island, the site of a magnificent series of early rock-cut temples within caves, lies about an hour off the coast opposite Bombay. Jim and I hired a private boat and ordered a fine picnic lunch, including a thermos of iced gin and fresh lime juice, Miss Leigh's stated favorite. But when the hour of departure arrived and we called her room at the Taj Mahal Hotel, she told us she hadn't slept well and felt too tired to make the Elephanta excursion. We went anyway; Jim had never been there, and the morning was a fine one. We consumed the contents of the picnic basket and drank up all the gin and lime juice and visited the caves—which we later used as one of the locations for our film *Bombay Talkie*.

That evening we had planned a lavish party in her honor and I was anxious, sitting in the boat on the way back, that she might not be well enough to come. That would have been a disaster. I had persuaded a society friend, Sunita Pitamber, to let me host it at her grand mansion and had invited some of the biggest film stars and socialites in the city. As soon as we returned from Elephanta I rushed to the hotel, where I found a recovered Miss Leigh making plans to see a cricket match and do some shopping. And the party? She would be there, she promised.

That night, the bejeweled film stars and socialites arrived—no one wanted to miss the chance to meet the famous actress—but the guest of honor remained stubbornly absent. Every time the doorbell rang, heralding a new arrival, my heart leaped in hope, then sank. The guests, too, began to look disappointed with each arrival who, at any other time, would have enjoyed more effusive welcomes. India's most famous leading man, Dilip Kumar, appeared and sat down to wait. Two hours passed, and I had all but lost hope, when suddenly she arrived with her Indian friends, the Palikivalas. She talked animatedly with other movie stars, but when anyone mentioned Scarlett O'Hara and *Gone With the Wind*, she spoke somewhat dismissively about

Vivien Leigh
finally arrives
at the party,
flanked by James
Ivory (crouching
deferentially, left),
Sunita Pitambar
(leaning over) and
Jabeen Jalil.

all that. *Gone With the Wind* had been made a long time before and she had done so much since. True, but most of the people there preferred the legendary Scarlett to her equally legendary Blanche Dubois. I regret that we never made our Afghan film with Vivien Leigh: Her health, never robust, had already begun its fatal decline.

Even before we had embarked on *The Householder*, Jim had been considering the idea of a film about a group of Indian traveling players, an idea that was cemented when we became involved with Shashi Kapoor. Shashi was married to the English actress Jennifer Kendal, daughter of actors Geoffrey Kendal and Laura Lidell, whose theater company, Shakespereana, toured India performing Shakespeare and other classic works. The story of their work and travels would inspire the subject of our second film, *Shakespeare Wallah*.

Ruth was approached to write the screenplay, and she drew loosely on Geoffrey Kendal's diaries to develop her story. Jim and I were in New York while Ruth was working on the script, and Jim and Ruth wrote to each other, proposing ideas and exchanging thoughts on the material, and thus they established the pattern for all our future collaborations.

I had expected Geoffrey and Laura to jump at the chance to play their counterparts on screen but, although they agreed to do the film, they had a low opinion of the art of film acting. Jennifer and Shashi, on the other hand, were very supportive of the idea, as was Jennifer's sister Felicity, who would go on to become one of the most popular and successful actresses on British stage and television.

Jim and I were eager to have Madhur Jaffrey in the film, and she was cast as the Indian movie star. Indian movie stars are, without exception, full-bosomed, wide-hipped, well-padded beauties. Madhur is slight and elegant. "Completely wrong." "It will be terrible." "A disaster!" were the reactions from some members of the production. But Madhur gave a brilliant performance and for that part won the Silver Bear for Best Actress at the Berlin Film Festival, the first award received by a Merchant Ivory film.

The advance of eighty thousand dollars we received from the sale of

The Householder to Columbia was reinvested in our ninety-thousand-dollar budget. We borrowed the rest, and deferred payments to Shashi and Ruth. It was a shoestring budget, and a very slender shoestring at that, even less than we'd had for our first film. The principles that we established then were the ones we would follow for the rest of our working lives: quality material, the finest actors, authentic locations and lots of hard work. We have never deviated from this philosophy.

Because the story of *Shakespeare Wallah* concerns a traveling company, we needed a variety of locations, and the Kendals helpfully suggested some of the places where they had performed. We became something of a traveling company ourselves as we shifted from Delhi to Lucknow, Kasauli, Simla, Alwar and Bombay.

An early scene in the film depicts a train journey as the acting troupe travels from one engagement to the next. I knew that we needed permission from the Ministry of Railways to shoot on a train, but experience had taught me that getting this permission would involve months and months of negotiations and money. So, because we were traveling from Delhi to our first location in Lucknow by train, we decided to dispense with the hassle of dealing with the Ministry of Railways. We reserved a whole compartment and shot the scene covertly. With little equipment, and Subrata Mitra's technique of bounce lighting, we managed to film the scene on our way to Lucknow.

Lucknow was a place I had wanted to visit since I was a boy. It is the capital of Uttar Pradesh and rose to prominence with the arrival of the Persian sheikhs during the reign of Emperor Akhbar in the sixteenth century. The city is renowned for its refined urban culture and cultivated, gracious manner. If you want to tease an Indian who is putting on airs, ask him if he comes from Lucknow.

In Lucknow, we filmed at the wonderfully ornate La Martinière, a fabulous structure built in 1795, by the French Claude Martin, a soldier of fortune working for the kings of Oudh. His builders freely mixed Moghul and

Felicity Kendal, the seventeen-year-old star of Shake-speare Wallah, made up and costumed for the opening scene of the film, shot at La Martinière, Lucknow, in 1964.

Corinthian columns, classical statues, Oriental turrets and rococo plaster work. Since the late 1800s, Martin's palace has functioned as a school, and Rudyard Kipling's fictional hero Kim was enrolled there.

I was keen to try the food of Lucknow because I had heard it was every bit as refined as its citizens. Once again I sourced the finest examples of this rich and extravagant cuisine which, unsurprisingly, was not exclusive to the grand restaurants. The finest kebabs in the city were available from a tiny stall where even the cream of Lucknowi society came for a meal of these truly irresistible creations: finely ground meat mixed with saffron, fennel seeds, peanuts, mace, cardamom and nutmeg, then wrapped in flaky *paratha* bread, which is rather like a croissant. Everyone on the set always got very excited when I announced I was going to Tunda's stall to get some kebabs.

One of the locations we needed was a palace: The maharajahs loved to entertain their guests with a performance of Shakespeare to establish their cultural credentials, and palaces featured frequently on the Kendals' performing route. Access to such places is difficult, but I had been told that the palace of Deeg at Bharatpur might be a possibility, so Jim and I went to meet Pratap Singh, the administrative officer. Mr. Singh was having lunch when we arrived, so I introduced myself to the guard and asked him to give Mr. Singh my Merchant Ivory Productions visiting card. The guard returned with the card and told us that Mr. Singh wasn't interested in buying any ivory. "No, no," I said. "I am not selling ivory. I am Ismail *Merchant* and this is James *Ivory*." The guard went back inside, and we heard Mr. Singh roaring at the guard: "I told you, damn fool, I don't want to buy any ivory, and you're bringing the card back again. Tell this ivory merchant to go away." Back and forth went the guard, so with no end to this misunderstanding in sight, I bypassed the guard and went straight in to see

Mr. Singh. But he was too disgruntled by this interruption of his lunch to agree to anything.

We couldn't get permission to shoot in Deeg but managed to gain access to the palace in Alwar, a small principality in the state of Rajasthan. The Maharajah of Alwar had two sons who looked after his affairs: The younger son was westernized and progressive; his older brother was very orthodox and religious. Unfortunately, it was the older brother who had to give his approval for everything relating to our shooting.

There were some very desirable artifacts in the palace, as well as priceless carpets and canopies, but in order to borrow them for the film, we had to ask the older brother, and access to him was limited because he always seemed to be at prayer. I would try to knock on the door of the room where he was doing his *puja* only to be shooed away by his aide. "You cannot disturb him while he is at prayer. He is communicating with *Bhagwan*," his aide would announce solemnly. With only four days to shoot this sequence, I was losing my patience with piety. I waited and waited. And would have been waiting still, but as I paced restlessly and angrily up and down, I accidentally tumbled over a huge *lotah*, an ornamental brass bowl that echoed thunderously as it charged along the floor of the long marble corridor. The door of the puja room opened, and the older son stood there holding his prayer thread and looked at me as if I had committed the gravest of crimes. He said nothing, and turned back and shut the door, his aide scurrying in with him. Well, I thought, that's the end of our shooting at the palace. But the aide came scurrying back—with permission to use anything we wanted. If only I had knocked over the lotah earlier.

Kasauli, high up in the hills of Punjab, is where the English in India spent their summers. Escaping the fiery heat of the cities, they created an unmistakably British ambience with typically Victorian architecture. The hotel we filmed in was the Alasia, a mock-Tudor, half-timbered affair that would not have seemed out of place in the English suburbs.

While we were in Kasauli we heard that a murder had recently taken place and that the body had disappeared. We were about to shoot a scene in which the funeral of an actor takes place, so I went to collect the coffin we had ordered from a carpenter. We fastened the coffin to the roof of the car and drove off to the location. Somewhere along the road a police car began to follow us, but because we were already late, I chose to ignore it rather than stop—until we were brought to a halt at a police checkpoint. What, the police wanted to know, was on top of our car? I told them it was a coffin. They could *see* it was a coffin, they said. They wanted to know what was *inside* the coffin. Murderers, on the whole, do not drive around the countryside with their corpses in coffins on top of cars, but this was India, where stranger things have been known to happen. I invited them to look inside. They seemed disappointed. What were we doing with a coffin on top of the car? they wanted to know. So I explained that we were shooting a film, which immediately aroused their suspicions because films in India are shot in studios and not in remote mountain villages. So I did what I was to do countless times: I told them we were making a film with Shashi Kapoor. By this time Shashi was a huge star, with a number of hit films to his name. The police immediately lost interest in the mislaid corpse and asked if there were any parts in the film for them.

It was while filming in Kasauli that I realized I might have made a great mistake in joining forces with Jim. Jim is a perfectionist, and while that is a very admirable quality, it is hugely inconvenient when you are making a film on very little time and even less money. I had attributed Jim's slow, methodical style of working on *The Householder* to his inexperience. Now I realized that that was the way he preferred to work. I would spend my days in frantic activity getting things organized, then I would rush to the set where time seemed to stand still while Jim and Subrata Mitra, our cinematographer—and another perfectionist—set the scene up: carefully, slowly, precisely. One shot would have been filmed when the schedule had called for six or seven. I would rage. Jim would ignore me—and still does. Of course when I see the rushes, I am always thrilled by the results of his painstaking approach, but on set, as the minutes and the dollars tick away, it's a very different story.

When we finished shooting, we took the film to Satyajit Ray to see if he would compose the score. He liked the film, and agreed to do it. When I told him we needed it in a week, he said that was very generous, and completed it in eight days. Ray suggested we should submit the film to the Berlin Film Festival and wrote to Dr. Bauer, the director of the festival, with a recommendation even though his own film, *Charulata*, was already entered in the competition.

Jim and I took our film to Berlin for Dr. Bauer's consideration, and we thought that instead of waiting in Berlin for his verdict, it would be a good time to go to Paris. Jim knew Paris well, but my only experience of the city had been when I had changed trains there on my first journey from Bombay to New York.

The Indian master film director Satyajit Ray (seen here, left, working at the music recording session) composed the film score for Shakespeare Wallah.

I had been traveling with a great deal of luggage on that occasion. In addition to clothes, books and farewell gifts, I had a large wicker hamper full of my mother's homemade pickles. Every Indian family produces its own characteristic pickle, and my mother believed that a meal without different varieties of her *aachar* was incomplete—not a meal at all. So she had made absolutely sure that for the duration of my studies in the United States I would not want for her pickles.

Porters seemed scarce at the Gare de Lyon, and when I finally found one he demanded his tip in advance, and he wanted it in dollars. I *had* dollars, but each one was already allocated to cover travel, accommodations, tuition, food and so on. My budget was extremely tight, and to start giving dollars away to porters would have unbalanced my carefully calculated finances. However, I also couldn't afford to lose what seemed to be the only porter at the Gare de Lyon.

I arrive at the Berlin Festival with Jennifer Kendal, one of the stars of Shakespeare Wallah, *in 1965.*

Pressebilderdienst Kindermann & Co

I was aware from all I had heard and read that the French enjoy the most distinguished cuisine in the world, and this gave me a brainstorm. The practice of bartering was common in Bombay so, painful though the sacrifice was, I opened my wicker hamper and offered the porter, in lieu of dollars, a jar of my mother's aachar, explaining to him in broken French that it was a special condiment prepared by my mother in India. Clearly the bartering system did not operate in the French capital because the porter continued to insist on dollars, unable to see the value of my mother's specially prepared pickles. I had no choice: There was a connecting train to catch. I gave the porter my dollars—three, I think—fewer than he demanded, but more than I could spare. To make up the shortfall I insisted he keep a jar of aachar. I was certain that once he had tasted this great speciality, he would regret not accepting his entire tip in pickles.

I was not well disposed toward the French, so I accepted Jim's suggestion of going to Paris from Berlin reluctantly. By the time we arrived there, I had developed an acute ear infection and was feeling very ill. Jim wanted to go

My Passage from India

62

to a concert at Notre Dame, and after the concert we walked over to the Ile St. Louis and had dinner at the Brasserie de l'Ile St. Louis, a wonderfully atmospheric, typically Parisian neighborhood brasserie where the steak and *frites* were so good I just about forgot my earache.

While we were in Paris we heard that *Shakespeare Wallah* had been selected for the Berlin Festival, and my attitude toward France softened, although I never imagined that I would grow to love the city so much that I would buy an apartment and set up an office there.

I invited everyone to Berlin for the festival. Shashi, Jennifer, Felicity, Madhur (who collected the Best Actress Award) all came, and of course Ray was there for his own film, although he seemed just as anxious about ours. At the press conference after the screening of *Shakespeare Wallah*, Michel Delahaye, the critic for the influential publication *Cahiers du Cinema*, delivered an overwhelming homage to the film, and his magazine offered to pay for the French subtitling of the film because they felt it should be released in France.

We were all staying at the Hotel Amzo, as was Gina Lollobrigida, who was also attending the festival, but none of us had been introduced to her. One day Gina shared the elevator with Shashi and seemed to take a great liking to him. She smiled at him, he smiled back. The next morning a huge bouquet of flowers was delivered to Madhur's room, and Madhur was very surprised indeed—and perhaps a little alarmed—to read such an effusive and affectionate note from Gina. Of course Indian names were so foreign to Gina that she couldn't distinguish between male and female, and how is an Italian expected to make any sense of Indian names anyway? So Shashi didn't respond to the flowers—and Madhur avoided Gina. It wasn't until the last night of our visit, at a party given by the festival, that a very vexed Gina—whose advances, presumably, were rarely spurned—made a point of confronting Shashi, and discovered her mistake. Poor Shashi was terribly disappointed that the confusion had caused him to miss such an opportunity.

The film was invited to the London Film Festival, and it was also shown at the New York Film Festival, with a very favorable response from both audiences and critics. Under those circumstances I never doubted the film would find a distributor but that, as I discovered, was not how the system worked. A starless film about an English theater troupe in India was not considered a commercial proposition, so no distributor in America was interested. I was surprised and disappointed by this reaction. The film had been well received wherever it had been shown. Why wouldn't it appeal to a wider audience? It was all a matter of money: the eternal battle between film as art and film as commerce. This was a war that never made any sense to me. If a film is good, regardless of its subject, then audiences will go to see it provided an opportunity is given to them.

I hired the Baronet cinema on Third Avenue, one of a number of art house cinemas owned in New York by Walter Reade, and we launched the film ourselves, gambling a sum of twenty thousand dollars, borrowed from Jim's father, on the advertising campaign, and giving the first performance as a benefit for UNICEF, attended by the Indian ambassador to the United Nations, Zsa Zsa Gabor, Huntington Hartford, the fashion designer Pauline Trigere and other celebrities. The gamble paid off. The film got a wonderful review in the *New York Times* and played for eight weeks at the Baronet. Reade-Sterling took it on for distribution, and Fox bought the film for some overseas territories. *Shakespeare Wallah* didn't set the box office cash registers alight, but it did enough business to give us a profile in the industry.

Jim had moved to a new apartment on East Fifty-second Street and, as I had no money to rent an office, I ran my business from there. It wasn't a very big apartment, nor were our activities very extensive, so the office didn't take up too much space. Most of the time, though, I would make phone calls from the offices of various friends and even arrange meetings in their offices. One such obliging friend was Nazrul Rehman, a handsome, distinguished Bengali who was head of the Indian Tea Board.

After the release of *Shakespeare Wallah*, however, we rented a tiny office on Madison Avenue because Paramount had agreed to finance the development of three films. *Vertical and Horizontal*, a comedy about psychoanalysis written by Lillian Ross, was an idea we were keen on, but Paramount considered the script anti-Semitic and thought it made fun of analysis, so after months of arguments and heartaches, the deal with Paramount ended.

By this time, the mid 1960s, the West had developed a fascination with Indian culture: Pop musicians studied the sitar with the great Indian maestro Ravi Shankar, and became followers of Maharishi Mahesh Yogi; amber-robed Hare Krishna devotees hummed their mantras on the streets of London and New York; and the smell of incense seemed to be everywhere—or maybe it was pot. The hippy movement found its expression in Indian mysticism and philosophy, and everything subcontinental was embraced by the mainstream youth culture.

The Guru (Uptal Dutt) and his disciple Tom Pickle (Michael York), an English rock star who seeks, like George Harrison, to find enlightenment and inspiration in India.

© 1969, Douglas Webb, Twentieth Century-Fox Film Corporation

Rita Tushingham gets last looks from the makeup department before shooting a scene in The Guru *as I look on.*

• • • • • • • • •

Begum Sahiba (Madhur Jaffrey) plots with the holy woman Mastani (Zohra Segal) to get rid of the guru's English groupie, Jenny.

And we were well placed to take advantage of the fashion. For some time Jim had been nursing the idea of a film about a great Indian musician and his devoted but untalented European disciple. After we changed the disciple into a pop star, Twentieth Century-Fox immediately commissioned the screenplay. Within twenty-four hours of reading Ruth's script, Fox gave *The Guru* the green light—and an $860,000 budget, more than I could ever have imagined. David Brown, who with Richard Zanuck was then head of production at Fox, called me personally: "It's a wonderful script, and you will make a wonderful film." We had never had such a speedy and unconditional response before—nor, for that matter, have we since. We felt we were the kings of the world.

We had no difficulty in engaging the English actors Michael York and Rita Tushingham for the parts of the pop star and his groupie girlfriend. They were the hottest stars of swinging-sixties cinema, and it was something of a coup for us.

The genesis of this film had been so smooth, so easy, so painless that something was bound to go wrong. And it did—in spades. For the part of the Indian maestro we cast Utpal Dutt, who had played the maharajah in *Shakespeare Wallah* and was among the most distinguished actors in India. Unfortunately, he was also a political activist and got himself arrested a few days before the shooting.

We were in the lobby of the Taj Mahal Hotel in Bombay discussing some last-minute adjustments to Dutt's costume when the police stormed in and dragged him off to Calcutta on charges of subversive Communist activities because he had put on Maoist plays in his native Bengal. I didn't have a clue about how to deal with this type of situation. Springing actors from prison was completely outside the scope of my experience. How, I wondered, would Fox react if I called them and told them our star was behind bars in a Bengali jail? I called Satyajit Ray to ask for his help.

The Guru's guru (Nana Palsikar) rebukes the film's guru master of the sitar, Ustad Zafar Khan, for his lack of dedication.

Ray immediately wrote on our behalf to Indira Gandhi, the prime minister, who was very supportive but reluctant to intervene on the grounds that it would put her under an obligation to the government of West Bengal. Ultimately, she did write to the West Bengal governor, and I flew to Calcutta to see what I could do with the authorities there. I remember the weather in Calcutta being sunny and warm, but I felt icy cold, as if I were in a morgue.

Douglas Webb

Because of all the wheels we had set in motion, the governor of West Bengal and his chief minister finally agreed to let me have Dutt back, but only on loan, as it were: As soon as he finished his work on our film, I had to guarantee to return him to Bengal to complete his sentence. I went to collect Dutt, who seemed completely unfazed by his experience. He told me he had spent his four days in jail practicing the sitar. By the time Fox found out and started sending anxious telegrams, Dutt was back in Bombay, so I could in good conscience tell them that all was well.

Our main location for *The Guru* was the fabulous sandstone and marble palace in the city of Bikaner in Rajasthan. We stayed in the guest quarters of the palace, as did the actors. I had always wondered what it would be like to live like a maharajah.

Soon after we arrived in Bikaner, a remote place in the middle of the Thar Desert, Michael York's girlfriend Pat (who would later become his wife) became gravely ill with an intestinal problem. The Maharajah of Bikaner's own doctor attended her and told us that if he didn't operate immediately, she would die. While we had absolute faith in the doctor, who had trained and practiced in the United States, we were less sanguine about the primitive facilities of the local hospital. But the situation was critical, so there was really no choice. The maharajah's doctor performed the operation, removing a large part of Pat's intestine that had become gangrenous.

We were due to move to our next location, Benares, in Uttar Pradesh, but had to leave Michael in Bikaner to stay with Pat, who was slowly recovering. Our shooting schedule had been disrupted by Dutt's arrest, and now, with Pat's illness, had to be completely reworked.

Benares is also known as Varanasi, and its original name, recorded in the twelfth century, was Kashi, which means "resplendent with divine light." It is one of the oldest cities in the world and has always been the religious capital of the Hindu faith. Devout Hindus make pilgrimages to Benares to shed their sins and purify themselves in the sacred water of the River Ganges, which comes down from the Himalayas and holds the power of salvation. The Hindu god Shiva is one of the presiding deities of this city, and it is be-

lieved that those who die there will be close to God in the other world. The Manikarnika, the burning ghat on the river bank—the chief cremation center—is where the corpses are immersed in the river before being placed on the funeral pyre. On either side of the Manikarnika, all along the bank, are the other ghats, the stepped landings, from where the pilgrims proceed into the river to bathe and purify themselves.

These spiritual associations add a haunting, mystical quality to the beauty of the city, and seem to inform many aspects of its cultural life, particularly the music. On my first visit there, when I went with Jim and Ruth to scout locations for the film, we were introduced to Girja Devi, a great Indian classical singer, who invited us to her house to sing for us and share a meal. She sang several devotional songs, accompanied by a small group of musicians playing tabla, *sarangi* and harmonium. I remember she wore a tan silk outfit with an immense skirt embroidered with gold thread along the hem that spread out around her in a circle of silk as she sat singing on the floor. Afterward we were served the most delicious vegetarian meal on individual silver *thalis*, or trays, with many different dishes, each in its own small silver bowl. We drank water and Coca-Cola with this feast, then walked back to our hotel down a long dark road, dazed with beautiful music and fine food.

Because Benares is largely a Hindu city, the food is strictly vegetarian and even the use of onions and garlic is frowned on as they are thought to inflame the blood. Despite these restrictions, the cuisine is astonishingly varied and quite superb. On that visit we also discovered Kachori Gulley, or the Lane of Fried Breads, where rotis, *kachoris* and *pooris*, light, puffy deep-fried breads, are the speciality. The breads can be served alone or with *aloo koda*, potatoes and pumpkin; or *aloo bhaji*, potatoes cooked with ginger and cumin seeds; and with *ghugni*, black chickpeas cooked with mustard and cumin seeds—all served on leaves. I also became addicted to the local sweets, especially the pancakelike *malpuas*, and *gari ka cheewra*, a heavenly confection of coconut flakes and powdered sugar.

But there was no time for such pleasures during the shooting, which we finally managed to complete despite the problems. The only high spot during those arduous months was when George Harrison of the Beatles came to India to record with Ravi Shankar, and they were photographed with Rita Tushingham. That picture made the cover of *Time* magazine, which was a great publicity boost for the film.

Vilayat Khan composed the score for the film, and he brought in a number of *ustads*, or maestri, from northern India to perform on the soundtrack at the recording studios in Bombay. When great musicians work together in India, it is traditional for them to sing each other's praises, quite literally, before they begin to perform. With so many ustads to praise and be praised, it soon became clear that this ritual would eat up our entire three-hour session without a note of music being recorded. I was told by the sound technicians to crack the whip with them, but there was simply no way of doing that without causing the most terrible offense. I tentatively suggested that perhaps the praises could be sung *after* the recording session. Vilayat Khan got the message. Although each recording session was approached with the greatest anxiety on my part, the result was one of our most beautiful scores.

Sadly, a beautiful score wasn't enough. The film had many fine qualities, but it just didn't work. After all we had been through, it was a disappointment, but there are no prizes for effort in filmmaking: A film either works or it doesn't. Fox wasn't too enthusiastic about the film, or about its chances at the box office, so they never distributed it properly or invested any money in promoting it. It was only after a lot of agitating on my part that they even agreed to show it at the 72nd Street Playhouse. Worse, by the time the film was released, the West's preoccupation with the subcontinent had played out, and *The Guru* was already passé.

I have always felt that success and failure are part of the same process, like life and death, and one has to accept that. Even though *The Guru* had not been a success, I knew I had done everything in my power to make the film work, and its subsequent fate was out of my control. So I went into the next film in a typically optimistic and ebullient mood. For me, there is no other way.

I decided to finance our next film, *Bombay Talkie*, privately, targeting merchant banks and businessmen on Wall Street who had an interest in cinema. Whenever I got wind of such individuals, I would maneuver into an introduction to them and make an offer I felt they couldn't refuse. Of course many did. But I never missed an opportunity, however unpromising, and eventually found an investor, Joseph Saleh, who put up the bulk of the $110,000 budget. Many years later Joe opened the Angelika Film Center in SoHo.

Saleh seemed an ideal match for us. An Iraqi/Jewish businessman who had made his fortune from real estate and other interests, he had once been an executive at Columbia Pictures and therefore had an insider's knowledge of how the system worked. Above all, he loved movies and, more to the point, got along very well with us. At one stage he even wanted to buy our company and put us under contract. The idea of having a guaranteed income was tempting, especially at a time when our survival was so precarious, but we preferred to hang on to our autonomy.

After the release of *The Guru*, we moved out of what had until then served as a makeshift office near Bombay's Liberty Cinema and into larger permanent premises in National House. In a way it was a kind of affirmation that, for all the ups and downs, we expected to be around for a long while. We have been there ever since.

Ruth had been working on an idea about an English writer of romantic fiction and her love affair with an Indian movie star. The opportunity of setting a film in the context of the Bombay film world and bringing in the wonderfully kitschy elements of that genre was irresistible. Long before I discovered Western films I was, like every other Indian, in thrall to the colorful, emotionally overwrought Bollywood films.

Jim and Ruth worked on the screenplay in their usual long-distance collaboration between New York and Delhi—how much easier our lives would have been if we'd had e-mail then—and by January 1970 *Bombay Talkie* was

ready for the cameras. We returned to what was becoming almost our repertory company of actors, with Shashi and Jennifer in the lead roles. Indeed, the Kapoors and the Kendals had become our second family. Just before we began shooting *The Householder*, Jennifer had given birth to their second child, Karan, within a couple of days of the birth of my nephew Nayeem and I regarded them both as my nephews.

And just as in all families, there were arguments and intrigues. Shashi had a lot of faith in this movie and invested some money in it in exchange for the rights to distribute the film in India. It was the beginning of his own production and distribution company, Film-Valas. But Shashi, who had yet to receive his deferred salary from *The Householder*, expected that money to be paid from the budget of *Bombay Talkie* before commencing work on the film. Unfortunately, we had ploughed our profits from *The Householder* into *Shakespeare Wallah*, and because we were making *Bombay Talkie* on a very tight budget, I simply didn't have the money to pay him. But Jennifer always had a soft spot for me and, seeing my predicament, lent me the money to pay Shashi. So, in effect, I used Shashi's own money to settle my debt with him. Of course I returned the money to Jennifer as soon as I was able to, but the whole transaction remained a secret from Shashi.

The opening sequence of *Bombay Talkie* is an archetypal Bollywood moment that came about from a dream Jim had had: a Busby Berkeley dance routine on the keys of a giant typewriter with Helen, the Anglo/Indian singing and dancing veteran of some five hundred Hindi films, leading the chorus line. We had the giant typewriter constructed in a Bombay studio—the first time, incidentally, we had ever shot at a studio rather than on location—but before the contractor could finish building it, he was arrested for some misdemeanor, and the job had to be completed by the assistant art director. After we finished shooting that scene we called the contractor to dismantle the set, but he was in prison and there was no indication of when he might be released. The studio was hassling us to vacate the sound stage because we were holding up other productions, so I had no choice but to call in a scrap merchant who came and demolished the set and charged us for

With Helen on the giant typewriter set of Bombay Talkie. *The dancers' movements on the keys type out fate. "It's very symbolic," says the director in the film.*

Bombay Talkie, released five years after Shakespeare Wallah, *took a closer look at the Bollywood film industry. It remains one of James Ivory's favorites.*

taking the broken pieces away. A few days later I was approached by a representative of Godrej, then the largest typewriter manufacturer in India, who had heard about our giant typewriter and wanted to use it for a commercial, offering a fee that would have covered a substantial part of our budget.

Jim and I had persuaded Ruth and Jhab to fly over from Delhi to see locations we had chosen in Bombay because I thought Ruth might like to see the places where her story would be set. We took them on a whirlwind tour of our sites and lost all track of time until they reminded me that they were about to miss their flight back to Delhi. I drove suicidally through Bombay's crowded streets, getting to the airport just as the steps were being removed from the aircraft. There was no time for the formalities of checking in, nor even dropping them off at the departure gate. I drove straight onto the runway and signaled wildly to the pilot to wait. Ruth and Jhab have never recovered from that trauma. Even today, when they are traveling entirely independent of Merchant Ivory business, they will set off for the airport at least three hours in advance.

As we gradually stumbled up the ladder of success, Jim's idea of comfort began to change. Although he had been happy to stay at my apartment on the previous occasions we had been in India, he now expected to receive accommodations commensurate with his status as an important director and insisted on a room at the Taj Mahal Hotel. This fine example of Victorian architecture faces Bombay Harbor, the Gateway of India, and each floor of the six-story building opens onto an interior veranda capped by a central dome and skylights. I wanted to use the Taj Mahal Hotel as one of the locations for the film, knowing, however, that at one time or another every filmmaker in India, including members of Shashi's family, had tried to shoot there, but permission had always been denied. My persistence paid off.

One of our scenes was an exterior night shot in front of the Taj, for which we arranged to have the street cleared and cordoned off. I arrived for the shooting and as I walked along the blocked-off street I remembered strolling along that area as a boy, never expecting that one day I would be in a position where I could take over that whole space and fill it with lights and

cameras and actors. Though not quite. One car remained stubbornly parked in front of the hotel, its owner not found. There was no time to waste, so I suggested we simply carry the car to the other side of the street. Subrata Mitra, our cinematographer, was intrigued by this idea because he thought it physically impossible and probably highly illegal. However, a dozen crew members managed to move the car, and we continued with our work . Many years later, when Mitra was honored at the Calcutta Film Festival, he recalled that incident at his press conference, still expressing wonderment.

In one of the ashram scenes we needed to show a home movie—something like today's home videos—of the swami, or holy man, on a visit to Hollywood. Jim remembered the 16-millimeter footage that I had shot in Hollywood with Agnes Moorehead attending my mahurat ceremony with a Hindu priest. We incorporated some new shots of the actor Pincho Kapoor, a Merchant Ivory regular who played the swami dressed in saffron robes, into our old footage of earnest-looking Californian matrons meeting the Mystic East. We also added the swami's self-approving narration, freshly

In my star turn as the Fate Machine Producer on the film set within a set for Bombay Talkie.

written by Ruth, to make a very enjoyable and effective sequence. This was a method we followed up a few years later in a more serious way in the film *Autobiography of a Princess*, in which we alternated fictional scenes with documentary footage throughout.

Bombay Talkie opened in New York in October 1970, and failed to make much money. The subjects we were interested in exploring—the Bombay film world, restless European women on the prowl in India, and mysticism—did not find a mass audience. Lately, however, video audiences, who seem more able to appreciate the somewhat melodramatic story, have rediscovered our fourth Indian feature. People seem fascinated by Bollywood now, as its products begin to merge with and influence Western movies more and more.

Jim and I never made a deliberate decision to extend the scope of our filmmaking beyond India; the process was more an organic one. We had sensed that there would never be more than a limited interest in films about India, and I think we both began to feel a need to stretch ourselves beyond our self-imposed limits. And, frankly, I was becoming increasingly frustrated by the red tape and bureaucracy that making films in India involved. We were ready to move on. It was just a matter of finding the right opportunity.

Such an opportunity presented itself when Mark Tully, the BBC's India correspondent, supported our idea of making a documentary on the Indian writer and polymath Nirad Chaudhuri, who was then living in England researching the life of the Sanskrit scholar Max Müller. Jim and I had met Chaudhuri, who was a great friend of Ruth and Jhab's, in India, and I felt we were qualified to do justice to this supremely erudite man. Chaudhuri, whose works include *The Autobiography of an Unknown Indian* and *The Continent of Circe*, had an extraordinary intellectual range: His knowledge of history, anthropology, linguistics, political science and sociology, among many other subjects, was as wide as it was deep, and he would certainly make a fascinating subject for a documentary.

Chaudhuri was seventy-six years old at that time, so I felt that if we didn't take the opportunity of documenting his life then, we might miss the chance forever. In fact, Chaudhuri lived on for another twenty-three years, dying at the age of 101. We had four days and ten thousand pounds for *Adventures of a Brown Man in Search of Civilization*, a title which came from one of the chapter titles of Chaudhuri's book *Passage to England*.

I wanted to ask the cinematographer Walter Lassally to shoot the film. We had been introduced to Walter by Subrata Mitra, who had invited him to a screening of *Bombay Talkie* in London. Walter was one of the most distinguished cinematographers in the world at the time, having shot *Tom Jones* and won an Academy Award for his brilliant work on *Zorba the Greek*. Jim's reaction to my suggestion was predictable. "Don't be ridiculous," he said. "He is probably too busy to work on a documentary, and you can't ask such a renowned cameraman to work on such a small film. Anyway, he wouldn't be interested in working with *us*." But I asked him anyway and he said yes, and soon became a regular member of our team and a very good friend. There is nothing to lose by asking, and I have become seasoned in this practice—although I still find a refusal very difficult to accept.

Jim had devised a number of settings in which to frame Chaudhuri—a visit to a graveyard, a don's study, a dinner party, a fitting at a tailor's, walking along an Oxford street—over which Chaudhuri extemporized provocatively with his usual wit and vigor on subjects as far ranging as Mozart and yoga. He clearly enjoyed every minute of it.

This was our first experience of working outside India, but shooting a film at Oxford University and Chiswick in London was really no different from shooting a film in India—apart from the weather.

I had asked Tony Korner, a friend of mine in New York, to recommend a tailor where we could shoot that sequence in the film, and Tony very generously introduced us to his own tailor on Saville Row. Tony could not have imagined how that simple exchange would disrupt his life over the next few years. I had met him in New York when I was trying to raise money for *Bombay Talkie* and had held a screening of *Shakespeare Wallah* for potential investors. Tony was then working as a banker, and he had close connections with India through his friendship with Karamat Jha, the son of the nizam of Hyderabad. Tony and Karamat had studied at Harrow.

Tony was tall, elegant and very good-looking. He belonged to a distinguished and wealthy banking family of Austrian origin that lived in London. Although Tony had taken up the family profession, his own passion was for the arts and, in particular, films. That and his ties with India forged the deep friendship that has now existed for more than thirty years. I remember meeting his formidable family, and Tony telling me later that his father had warned him to stay away from the "oriental adventurer," suspecting I intended to relieve Tony of his money, art collection and all his possessions to finance my crazy schemes. Well, I have been trying for the past thirty years, but I have failed to make even a dent in his fortune. I still persist, unmoved by Tony's insistence that he is virtually on the breadline—a claim that might carry more weight but for the constantly multiplying art collection in his home.

Although I have yet to part Tony from his money, I did, much to his family's horror, part him from banking. Tony had become intrigued by the possibility of making a documentary on Helen, the Anglo/Indian singing and dancing star whom we had featured in our film *Bombay Talkie.* Rather than talk Tony out of the idea, I encouraged him to pursue it. Our documentary on Chaudhuri had been very well received, and I felt confident we could also make an interesting film of *Helen, Queen of the Nautch Girls,* so we returned briefly to Bombay in January 1971. I scraped together seventeen thousand dollars, Jim composed a commentary, and Tony directed and narrated the film.

We used a number of film clips to illustrate Helen's performances, which probably seemed like the height of kitsch to Western audiences, but the clips were representative of the most popular Hindi films of the time. Helen was filmed in a number of situations talking about her work and her life and what she might do when her performing days came to an end. The film was a vibrant and compelling observation of an aspect of Indian culture that had not yet been explored: the hugely popular appeal of the extravagant roman-

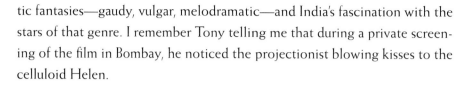

tic fantasies—gaudy, vulgar, melodramatic—and India's fascination with the stars of that genre. I remember Tony telling me that during a private screening of the film in Bombay, he noticed the projectionist blowing kisses to the celluloid Helen.

Tony then joined us in New York as associate producer of *Savages*, our first American film, which we shot in the spring of 1971 near Scarborough, on the Hudson River in Upstate New York.

The disappointing performance of *Bombay Talkie* at the box office did nothing to diminish Joseph Saleh's faith in us. He continued to champion our work and agreed to finance *Savages*, which, given the single location, nonunion crew, and off-Broadway actors, I thought we could make for $150,000. I was a little wide of the mark. It ended up costing $350,000. The figure just kept rising despite all the concessions made to the film's low budget: Tony turned his hand to designing the elaborate masks we needed for the production, and our cinematographer, Walter Lassally, worked for a very modest fee plus, optimistically, a share of the profits. That Walter agreed to this derisory deal came as no surprise. As an Academy Award winner he was much in demand and could pick and choose his jobs, but I'd gotten to know him during our previous film, and I realized that, like us, he was motivated by interesting work rather than the size of the paycheck.

The lean budget led to long working hours and created generally demanding conditions for the whole unit. While no one actually complained, I was nevertheless aware that morale was low, and it upset me. I knew that no one would ever get rich working on a Merchant Ivory movie, so I had always tried to compensate for that by making the experience itself as pleasurable as possible. I have never taken anyone's contribution to a film for granted, and I wanted to show the *Savages* unit how much I appreciated their hard work and commitment, so I decided to cook for them. One Friday night I hauled up to the location great bags of rice and lentils, minced beef and chicken, boxes of vegetables and fruit and the best wine I could afford, and set to work making *keema*, chicken cooked in yogurt, fragrant rice, lemon dal and spiced cauliflower and potatoes.

I had announced the dinner on the call sheet, but I didn't think anyone took it seriously. As far as I knew, it was unprecedented for a film producer to roll up his shirtsleeves and cook for his cast and crew, so the novelty of the occasion drew everyone to the dinner. It was such a success—people still talked about it days later—that I decided to repeat it the following week, and the week after that. It certainly achieved the desired effect of boosting everyone's spirits. Thus began the tradition of the end-of-week curry party that continues to this day. People have come to expect it almost as a condition of their contracts, and I hate to think what the consequences might be if I failed to deliver.

Savages was selected for the newly established Directors' Fortnight at the Cannes Film Festival in 1972, and enjoyed tremendous success. The French critics loved the film and, even though it was not in the main competition, it became the must-see entry and the most-talked about film at the festival. It was the other critics who deemed the film a sophomoric exercise.

The film received a similar reception at the London Film Festival, and it swiftly found a British distributor. In the United States, however, nobody wanted to hear about it. American distributors were cautious about taking on a film that didn't seem to fit an identifiable genre. I persuaded Joe Saleh that we should open the film ourselves, so we took the Baronet Theater in New York, where *Shakespeare Wallah* had played so successfully. But *Savages* had a harsher fate in store; the critics gave it a merciless panning, with the exception of *The New Yorker* and the *New York Times*, which credited the film with some redeeming features. After five weeks we decided to cut our losses and move on. (*Savages* acquired a cult reputation on the college circuit, however, and even today has a loyal following.)

For me, moving on involved returning to India, not as a result of any disenchantment with our first experience of working in America, but because I had stumbled on the opportunity to direct a short film.

I had been approached by Sajid Khan, once a popular child actor in India—Satyajit Ray thought he was the best natural child actor he'd ever seen—who had come up with an idea about a day in the life of a vagrant boy

Sajid Khan, who had been a child star in India, plays the boy who holds conversations with a statue of Mahatma Gandhi.

on Bombay's Juhu Beach. The broad littoral of Juhu, about twelve miles from the city, is the first glimpse of India those flying into Bombay will see. As a child I used to visit Juhu, taking the bus to the beach and walking among the people there. Sometimes I would buy coconut water and potato patties from one of the food stalls and just sit and watch the entertainers: the snake charmers, the acrobats and the monkey wallahs. It was a world I knew from my childhood.

Mahatma and the Mad Boy records a day in the life of a destitute adolescent who lives on the beach, begging or stealing an existence with the help of his pet monkey and conversing philosophically with a statue of Mahatma Gandhi. The Indian writer Tanveer Farooqui had prepared the script, and Subrata Mitra agreed to be my cinematographer. Sajid Khan, of course, was ideally suited to play the endearing Mad Boy who lives by his wits.

Mitra has a great sense of what is real, and he suggested that the statue of Gandhi that we were having made should be struck in a pensive, thoughtful pose so that he would appear to be listening to the boy, and the audience could almost believe there was a relationship between the boy and the statue. It was an inspired idea that was realized by the art director Bansi Chandragupta.

I reckoned we could shoot the film in about five days at a cost of thirty thousand dollars. I didn't bother to waste time looking for a financier: I knew no one would be interested in a short film on such an esoteric subject, so we financed the film ourselves. The First Commandment of filmmaking is never to invest your own money in a project, but if we had obeyed that law, we never would have gotten started. Few, if any, of our films can be pitched successfully to a studio or other backer. I frequently have to come up with our own money to start the ball rolling on a film that I passionately believe in but no one else does.

We shot the film in August of 1972, during some stormy weather that gave us a wonderfully dramatic backdrop: huge, billowing gunmetal-gray clouds that cast ominous shadows over the beach, and seemed to be appropriate reflections of the political and social elements in the story. It was the overcast skyscape that gave me the idea of using Vivaldi's "Winter" Concerto as the musical theme of the film. I had already decided that I wanted the music to be played on the *sarangi,* an Indian stringed instrument with a haunting quality that I felt would give a tone like a cry from the heart to the boy's plight. I approached the great sarangi player Sultan Khan to discuss adapting the Vivaldi piece to this instrument. Together with his musicians he adapted the "Winter" Concerto, drawing on an Indian *rag* to create one of the most haunting and moving melodies. We recorded the music in a single session on the last night of shooting, but we had to rerecord it later because of technical problems. Sadly, Khan was then unavailable, but another brilliant exponent of that instrument, Ram Narayan, stepped in when we recorded the score in London.

Film directors are always warned not to work with children or animals: For *Mahatma and the Mad Boy* I had Sajid, who, though no longer a child, had been formed as a child actor, and a monkey, who, though trained, had his own ideas about the performance he should give and paid little attention to his director.

When we came to shoot the scene where a politician arrives by car at the beach to campaign for election, we discovered that the actor playing the part of the chauffeur lacked one essential qualification for the role: He couldn't drive. There was no time to waste so I threw off my director's hat—and my producer's hat—put on the chauffeur's hat and got behind the wheel, mumbling directions sotto voce to the actor in the backseat playing the politician.

Mahatma and the Mad Boy was sold to the BBC in England and to PBS in the United States, and it received highly favorable reviews when it was shown—very gratifying for a rookie director.

It wasn't the first time, nor the last, that I appeared in front of the cameras in one of our films. While we were shooting *The Householder*, Jim needed someone in the background of a shot, and in order to save time—I knew how long it would take him to find just the right person—I said I would do it. In *Shakespeare Wallah* I had another fleeting appearance as the theater manager. By the time we made *The Guru*, I had graduated to a real part, as the master of ceremonies at a beauty contest. In *Bombay Talkie* I was cast, imaginatively, as the producer of the dance number on the giant typewriter. Even less of a stretch was my appearance in *Hullabaloo Over Georgie and Bonnie's Pictures*, where I fly into a terrifying rage and smash up a telephone, something I do in the office frequently. I have been a peasant in *Heat and Dust* and an elaborately costumed nawab in *Jefferson in Paris*, unrecognizable behind an

Me in London, at the theater where Mahatma and the Mad Boy *played.*

extravagant walrus moustache. Like Alfred Hitchcock, I have made a cameo appearance in most of our films. I suppose there must be something of the ham in me because I love getting in front of the camera, and clowning around with the other actors.

In fact, during my final year at St. Xavier's I was asked by the distinguished theater director Al Kazi to play one of the two lovers in an Urdu adaptation of Molière's *Les fourberies de Scapin*. I accepted instantly, even though the play's rehearsals were scheduled at the time I was frantically organizing my trip to New York, so I frequently arrived late—and sometimes missed them entirely. I was severely reprimanded by Al Kazi, who saw no hope as far as my acting career was concerned. Nevertheless, the play was a great success and I was praised for my performance. Even Al Kazi had to revise his opinion of my potential. "I see there is a glimmer of talent," he told me. "But you need discipline." Alas, I would remain a stranger to discipline, so my professional acting debut was also my farewell to the stage.

More than eighteen months passed before we got behind the cameras again, and then made up for lost time by shooting two films in the same year. We had not been idle during 1973, however. Tony Korner and I had been in India gathering the bulk of the material for a documentary about India's royal families that we had been planning since 1971. We used our various trips to India over that period to shoot some interviews with the descendants of the maharajahs, and assemble archival film footage, largely from the royal princes' decaying home movies made between the 1920s and the 1940s.

Tony had been issued an ultimatum by his father: Return to the bank or risk being disinherited from his fortune. Neither option, understandably, appealed to Tony, so he negotiated a concession from his father: a year's leave to go to Rajasthan to finish what we had started, then he would go back to banking. Eventually, though, Tony would turn his back on banking forever. He is now the publisher of *Artforum*, the leading periodical on contemporary art.

While we were in Jodhpur, an ancient city situated on the edge of the Thar Desert in Rajasthan, I asked Ruth and Jim to join us. I have a great fondness for that city and thought they would enjoy the experience, but had I known how close I was to getting us all killed, I would probably have recommended they remain at home.

The state of Rajasthan was once known as Rajputana, which translates as "abode of kings." It is an area steeped in history, legend, folklore and romance, and its people still adhere to the courtly refinements of courtesy and culture, and nowhere more so than in Jodhpur. Dominated by the monolithic Meherangarh Fort, rising some four hundred feet above the city, Jodhpur contains a wealth of historic treasures, not the least of which is Umaid Bhawan Palace, the last of the great Indian palaces to be built. It is believed to be the largest, with the building alone covering three and a half acres of the twenty-six-acre site. Designed by the English architect Henry Lanchester, the sandstone building was constructed between 1929 and 1943 and represents one of the finest examples of art deco architecture and design.

Umaid Bhawan, in common with most Indian palaces, now functions as a hotel, albeit in a very discreet way, with an impressive guest list that has included many distinguished names, from Jacqueline Onassis to Peter O'Toole. Bapji, the present maharajah of Jodhpur, retains one wing of the palace as his personal residence, and it was there that Ruth, Jim and I were summoned to join Bapji, his family, and their English friend, Douglas, for dinner one night during our stay.

I had known Bapji from an earlier visit when we had approached him about material for the documentary, and he had been extremely accommodating, generously offering us the reels of archive film of durbars and pig-sticking and tiger shooting that were rotting in the basements of his palace. Alarmingly, this was all on nitrate film, which is highly combustible and could have burned down the whole monumental place. Too dangerous to use in that state, it was transferred to safety film as soon as we could manage it. From that first visit to Jodhpur a friendship grew with Bapji, a very gracious, intelligent and unaffected man, and he had been part of our entourage at the Cannes Film Festival when we had shown *Savages*, although I don't think he enjoyed the occasion very much because he suffered from a severe bout of flu from the day he arrived until the day he left. Bapji was in much better spirits over dinner in Jodhpur, where we also had the pleasure of meeting his wife, Hemlata, to whom he had recently been married.

While we were enjoying this great Rajasthani feast, Bapji's illegitimate brother, Tutu, suddenly burst into the dining room armed with a huge ceremonial sword he slashed wildly at us. He lunged at Bapji with it, yelling incomprehensible threats as he tried to slice off Bapji's head. Bapji's great-great-aunt, Baiji, rose from her seat, and Tutu immediately turned the sword on her. "If you move," yelled Tutu, "this sword will slice off your head too." Hemlata threw herself in front of Bapji, screaming at Tutu that he would have to kill her first. Bapji's mother, who had been showing us some rare family jewels, seemed more concerned about the priceless diamonds that had scattered across the floor. The servants, anticipating a bloodbath, all disappeared in a flash while we were left to the mercy of a madman. It was like a scene from the past that should have been played out at the medieval fort across the city.

We knew that Tutu was slightly deranged and that he bore a bitter resentment toward Bapji, who was a legitimate son, but we never expected anything like a violent attack. We were paralyzed with surprise and horror. Jim and I could do nothing but stare bug-eyed at Tutu's thrashing sword, wondering if it would strike us. It was Ruth, slight, diminutive Ruth, who finally took Tutu on. "How dare you come in like this," she screamed at him. "Get out at once!" Well, of course he didn't. So Ruth started calling for the servants to come and take him away, which they eventually did, leaving us all severely shaken.

Ruth's fragile appearance and self-effacing manner are deceptive. Even-tempered and mild, as a rule, she can be very determined and strong willed under certain circumstances. Confronted with unpleasantness or menace, she behaves like a tigress, and tolerates no nonsense from anyone.

Much later we heard that Tutu had been beheaded and his body chopped to pieces by the local mafia—a brutal end to an ongoing family

Tony Korner visited us on location for In Custody, *my feature-film directorial debut.*

. . . .

Autobiography of a Princess *incorporates into its narrative rare nineteenth-century royal portraits. Mangal Singh of Thana, maharajah of Alwar (reigned 1874–1892).*

feud by ancient methods that sometimes resurface in Rajasthan.

On that trip we also visited the medieval city of Jaisalmer, deep in the desert about three hundred miles from Jodhpur. Once a smuggler's paradise, the city has hardly changed in hundreds of years, and it is a visual feast of architecture: The facade of every building, each constructed from the local yellow stone that shimmers like gold in the fierce sunlight, is embellished with exquisite carvings, and filigree so delicate it seems to drape like the finest lace. While we were there, we came across a wonderful singer who was eighty years old and had the most compelling and photogenic face. The combination of her haunting melodies and expressive features seemed to be made for the cameras. We filmed her, of course, adding that footage to the rest of the magpie accumulation that would surface again in our film *Autobiography of a Princess*.

The idea for that film came from the long conversations we had in Jodhpur with Baiji, who, as a royal princess, had been educated in England and Switzerland and was then expected to return to Jodhpur and go into purdah, or seclusion. The intended documentary was abandoned, and Jim and Ruth proposed instead the story of an Indian princess self-exiled in London. The archive footage we had uncovered would be used to show the world she had left behind.

Using the material we had filmed, the interviews, the archive reels and a lot of notes from Jim, Ruth conceived the story of *Autobiography of a Princess*. We all agreed that Madhur Jaffrey was born to play the part of an imperious, temperamental Indian princess. Ruth's script also called for an Englishman once attached to the royal court, so we considered Ralph Richardson, John Gielgud and Laurence Olivier for that part. I felt that James Mason would also be good in the role, but Jim and Ruth weren't keen on the idea; they considered him far too glamorous. I thought they should reserve judgment until they met him, so we arranged to have dinner together at the Dorchester Hotel in London. The meeting went well, but Jim remained doubtful until the day of the shoot when Mason transformed himself into the character Cyril Sahib, the modest, intelligent Englishman of that world. Even his voice seemed to change.

Madhur, of course, was in her element as the spoiled, temperamental princess. All she lacked were the jewels. Jim and I felt that costume jewelry just wouldn't be right. We had a modest budget of sixty thousand pounds, so the kind of glittering gemstones appropriate to an Indian princess were entirely beyond our means. The pieces we needed were tantalizingly close: They were displayed in the windows of Garrards of London, the crown jewelers on Regent Street. I toyed with the idea of smashing the glass, grabbing the jewels and stashing them in the apartment in Holland Park that was our location for the film.

Our hearts were set on those emeralds. I decided to pay a visit to Garrards to see if we could borrow the jewels. Jim and Madhur insisted on coming with me, probably terrified that if Garrards refused, I might be tempted to take the jewels anyway. As luck would have it, the public relations executive at Garrards actually recognized our names. She was a film buff who had seen and admired *Shakespeare Wallah,* and she was eager to help us. I pointed to the emerald-and-diamond necklace with matching ring and earrings, valued at a quarter of a million pounds, and a very, very expensive diamond-studded wristwatch, for which we could offer no collateral whatsoever. The public relations executive gulped, but agreed to let us borrow the pieces on condition that a representative from Garrards and two security guards would be assigned to cover the jewels at all times. This was absolutely fine by me, though less fine by Madhur, whose every move was shadowed by two hulking men. They accompanied her everywhere, even to the powder room. "What do they think I'm going to do with them?" snapped Madhur at one point, "*flush* them away?"

Within weeks of wrapping the six-day shoot of *Autobiography of a Princess*, we were in California on the set of our next film, *The Wild Party*, set in the Hollywood film world of the 1920s and starring Raquel Welch. In a sense, this was the realization of those dreams I had had back in college when I planned to make movies with the biggest and most glamorous stars in the business. Raquel Welch was without rival the biggest and sexiest star in Hollywood at that time.

In 197⌐ Jim bought a large house in Claverack, about two hours from New York City in the Hudson Valley, using the money he had been given when a property he had inherited from his father in California had been condemned for a freeway. Built in 1805 for a local politician, it was a huge and desperately neglected mansion, but it appealed to Jim, who saw how it could be restored to its original grandeur. I felt it was a little unwise to get involved in such a massive project, but Jim had made his mind up. It took more than twenty years—and I hate to think how many dollars—before the renovation was complete.

The following year Ruth decided to divide her time between India and New York, spending the greater part of the year in the United States, where she took an apartment in our building in Manhattan. Her youngest daughter, Firoza, a gifted pianist, was enrolled at the Mannes College of Music on the Upper East Side. It was through them that I met Richard Robbins, Firoza's piano teacher and director of the Mannes Preparatory Division and, as I discovered, a brilliant musician and composer in his own right. Dick suggested making a documentary on the college and its teaching methods, and so we put together *Sweet Sounds*, an engaging record of a group of preschool children and their first attempts to make music.

I was very much impressed by the way Dick connected with the children, and by his passion for music. It was a passion I shared, and I soon developed a rapport with this warm and unassuming man. Dick had studied in Vienna and, had he chosen, could have pursued a career as a concert pianist, but he disliked the limelight and was happier to inspire and guide and pass on his knowledge to future musicians. Within a few years I would persuade him to leave teaching and concentrate on composing film music, something I think he is still ambivalent about despite the two Academy Award nominations and the many awards he has received for his work.

After *Roseland*, our film set in New York's famous dance palace, we returned to India in 1978 for *Hullabaloo Over Georgie and Bonnie's Pictures*, a film that had been commissioned by Melvyn Bragg for the *South Bank Show*, a new arts program for London Weekend Television that Bragg was presenting. Bragg, a British novelist who had once interviewed Ruth for the BBC, approached her to offer a film on a subject of our choice to be financed by LWT provided it had a connection with the arts. We tossed various ideas around, and finally settled on the subject of collecting Indian miniature paintings, something that Jim had been doing for twenty years since his interest had been aroused while he was making *The Sword and the Flute*.

Jim's interest in this subject had aroused mine. I knew little about Indian miniature painting until we made *The Householder*, when Jim would spend all his free time visiting dealers, and I tagged along. We would go into tiny shops where shady dealers—or perhaps they just looked shady—sat behind shuttered windows. They would bring out musty-smelling bundles, cloth bags tied with string that they would carefully unwrap to reveal miniature treasures. Gradually I got hooked and began collecting in a modest way. Jim has a scholarly knowledge of these paintings. I don't: I go by instinct—if something speaks to me, I buy it.

The premise of the story that Ruth came up with—after so much agonizing that at one point she wanted to give up on the whole affair—involved the games two rival art collectors engage in to get their hands on a priceless collection of Indian miniatures belonging to a young maharajah and his sister. We approached the British stage actress Dame Peggy Ashcroft to play the part of the English collector, and were thrilled when she accepted because she made very few films, preferring to work in the theater.

Eight years had passed since we had made *Bombay Talkie*, and six since I had made *Mahatma and the Mad Boy*, and both Jim and I were ready to return. I had, of course, visited India frequently during those years to see my parents, who were never inclined to visit me in England or America. Sometimes they thought about it, and even talked about it, but they seemed happier to stay in the familiarity of their own surroundings, so they never made the effort to travel abroad.

Mary Ellen Mark

Art dealer Shri Narain (Saeed Jaffrey) tries to interest hard-to-please Lady Ghee (Dame Peggy Ashcroft) in his wares.

In the time since we had last worked in India, costs had risen substantially, and I had seriously underestimated the budget. I had to find ways to cut expenses, and I reasoned that, because the film was contemporary, it was possible we could begin by dispensing with a costume designer and find what we needed in the bazaars and shops. I knew, however, that an actress of Dame Peggy's stature would expect to have her wardrobe assembled professionally, and there was also a short flashback sequence within the film that required costumes for the 1920s. My cavalier attitude toward the matter of costumes clearly fell rather short of reality.

Fortunately, at this point Jenny Beaven came into our lives through a very tangled web. Jenny had studied theater design at the Central School, and was beginning to make a name for herself as a very gifted costume designer, particularly in opera and ballet. In fact, she had just designed the costumes for a new production of *Carmen* at the Royal Opera House. She had known Nick Young, one of the researchers for the *South Bank Show* and an associate producer of our film, since they had attended dance classes together as children, and Nick suggested using Jenny to put together Dame Peggy's wardrobe for the film. Jenny was introduced to Dame Peggy, and they got on so famously that when the time came to leave London for India, Dame Peggy, who was then seventy years old and a little concerned about undertaking this Indian adventure alone, proposed that she should trade in her first-class air ticket for two economy-class tickets and take Jenny along with her. Jenny readily agreed, blissfully ignorant of what she was about to get into.

It soon became clear that a costume designer was indispensable to the film, and Jenny gradually assumed those duties, largely because I treated the matter as a fait accompli. Early in the mornings I would take Jenny in a rickshaw to the bazaars of Jodhpur, stopping first at a *halwaii*, a sweetmeat seller, where we would breakfast on *jellabis*, deep-fried, doughnutlike sweets, and glasses of cool milk. The smell of the freshly cooked jellabis was so irresistible that we couldn't wait for them to cool off, burning our fingers and lips

Bonnie (Aparna Sen) playing one of her ancestors who was kept in purdah.

Mary Ellen Mark

as we wolfed them down steaming hot. Then we would wander through the bazaar, and I would ask her to pick out the clothes for a particular actor or a particular scene. And it didn't end there. We decided that Jenny would be perfect in the small part of the governess, and when we needed someone to recite a poem, we decided that Jenny, with her beautiful speaking voice, was the one to do it.

Jenny took it all in stride, even though I don't think we ever paid her more than a per diem, but, given her many and varied functions on the film, she ended up with a great number of credits. Although she had never intended to work in films, Jenny went on to become one of the most distinguished costume designers in the business, working with us many times and, together with codesigner John Bright, collecting two Academy Awards for *A Room with a View* and *Howards End*.

We shot the film in Jodhpur, making use of some fabulous locations, including the massive fort and Umaid Bhawan Palace, where we stayed. Bapji was enormously hospitable and helpful to us—and behaved with the utmost courtesy when we almost burned his palace down during filming. For the scene in which the miniature paintings appear to be on fire, we prepared bundles of rags soaked in kerosene, enough bundles for several takes if necessary. This was an interior scene, so we took the precaution of having a few fire extinguishers at hand, not so much because we expected to set the palace alight, but because we needed to put out the fire after shooting the scene.

Unfortunately, on the first take the flames spread from one kerosene-soaked bundle to the next, and before we even had a chance to react, the fire took hold. The flames leaped out of the window, and the exterior shot looks as though the whole palace was on fire. Everyone in the unit was shocked: We had come to shoot a film at this historic site and were about to leave it a pile of ashes. Some fast-thinking assistants on the crew grabbed the extinguishers and eventually managed to put the fire out, but not before the room suffered quite a lot of damage.

Jim felt we had behaved badly, and he saw no difference between us and the characters in the film who were intent on raiding the palace of its trea-

sures no matter what the cost. Bapji, on the other hand, regarded this as nothing more than an unfortunate accident and, generously, dismissed the incident. Terrible things always seemed to happen to us in Jodhpur, but it remains one of my favorite places, and one of very special memories.

Jim had read very little of Henry James's work, a fact that surprised Ruth when she came to know about this omission. She felt that Jim would be drawn naturally to the characters and themes of James's work, and she urged him to read all the novels, starting with *The Europeans*. Jim complied, systematically reading the books over the next few years, and becoming as much of an admirer of James as Ruth was. The impulse to film *The Europeans* probably came initially from Ruth, but Jim was also a strong advocate of the project. He would watch British-made adaptations of James on television and wonder why no American company had thought of filming his work. I soon found out when I began looking for financing. The Americans weren't remotely interested—they regarded James as unfilmable—so I had to raise the money from European sources, chiefly from the National Film Finance Corporation in England.

Contrary to the expectations of craven American financiers, audiences responded very positively to the film, which became our most successful up to that point, and it was accepted into the main competition at Cannes. *The Europeans* did respectable business, enough to allow us to move from our cramped offices on Columbus Circle to marginally less cramped offices in the Fisk Building on West Fifty-seventh Street, where we have been ever since. As our operation grew we knocked through to the adjoining office, then when that, too, became impenetrable with files and boxes and film reels, we moved to a larger suite.

After we returned to the United States from Cannes, Jim heard that Channel 13 was working on adaptations of three John Cheever stories, and he approached them about the possibility of directing *The Five Forty-Eight* for

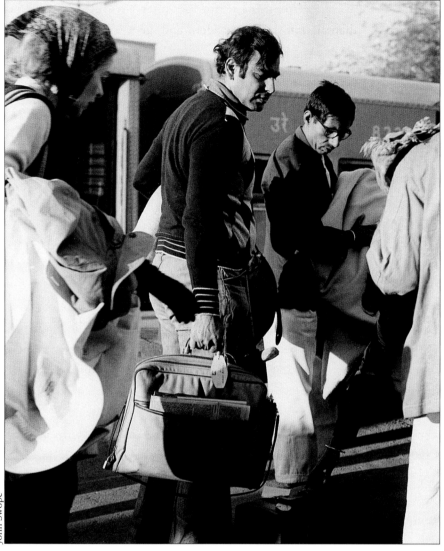

John Swope

*On the go as usual,
at a rail station in
Rajasthan in
the early 1970s.*

no better reason than he thought it might be fun to work on a contemporary thriller.

Although Ruth, Jim and I work closely together on films that appeal to us equally, our collaboration is not exclusive, and sometimes we work independently of each other. If Ruth and Jim do not share my enthusiasm for

something, then I do not press the matter any further with them, and look elsewhere for collaborators. And Ruth and Jim know that if they can't infect me with their enthusiasm for a particular project, then I won't take it on. The burden of raising funds for a film and then putting the whole package together is so enormous and so draining that I need to be overwhelmed with passion for it before I can begin to persuade financiers and actors to participate in the piece, or undertake the sacrifices and risks it might require.

One of the many such examples I can recall about the commitment involved was when I was trying to raise a $750,000 budget for *The Europeans*. The response was so negative that when the German television company Polytel showed just a glimmer of interest in the project and suggested they might be prepared to put up $50,000, I immediately flew to Cannes to meet with them. This would be the first investment in the film and, even though the amount was tiny, I desperately needed to secure that seed money so we could proceed. I checked into the expensive Hotel du Cap, where the Germans were staying, even though I could not afford it and had no idea how I would pay the bill. I had to create the impression that I was meeting the Germans on their level. The Germans committed, which meant I could get the film to the next stage—and pay the hotel. You can only engage in that kind of nerve-breaking activity if your dedication to a project is total.

While Jim was involved with his thriller, Ruth was writing the screenplay for *Jane Austen in Manhattan*, one of the most bizarre projects we were ever to take on. During a party given for us at London's Garrick Club after the screening of *Hullabaloo Over Georgie and Bonnie's Pictures*, Melvyn Bragg mentioned that London Weekend Television had bought the rights to a newly discovered unpublished play by Jane Austen, and he thought we were the perfect team to film it for television. Of course we jumped at the chance. Then we found out that it wasn't a complete play at all, just some fragments that Austen had written as a child, and I couldn't even begin to imagine how we would ever make anything of it. Jim wanted to back out of the whole thing, but it was too late because Bragg had made the deal, which he shrewdly announced to the press—before we'd even seen the material.

Ruth, on the other hand, was intrigued by the possibilities of experimenting with these incomplete fragments. And I was keen to work with Melvyn Bragg again because it gave me the opportunity to use all his facilities at London Weekend Television, including his office and his telephone. I had absolutely no right to appropriate Melvyn's office in this way, but we couldn't afford one of our own in London, and I needed a place from which to operate. In fact, we couldn't even have stayed in London had it not been for Tony Korner, who had bought a lovely apartment in Kensington that he allowed us to use whenever we were in town.

Quartet, which we shot in Paris in 1980, was the first of many films we would make in France. It was also indirectly initiated by Ruth, who had introduced Jim to the novels of Jean Rhys. Jim had always been interested in the idea of making a film in Paris, and the 1920s setting of the novel particularly appealed to him. For me, a long stay in Paris was the chance to discover a city that I had barely glimpsed on many business visits there. I knew from those visits that I loved the place: the people; the food; the markets, and especially Les Halles, which reminded me of Crawford Market in Bombay.

But even as I was in the throes of producing this very ambitious film in a strange city, I was also setting up a project of my own in Bombay. As soon as shooting wrapped in Paris in December, I was on my way to India to begin *The Courtesans of Bombay*, a film I had been thinking about for many years. The subject of this docudrama was Pavan Pol, the self-contained community of courtesans and a unique part of Bombay life.

The courtesans practice the traditional arts of singing and dancing, and are a required pres-

The courtesans entertained their male clients by dancing both to popular music of the day and to classical Indian music.

Karin Kapoor

ence at weddings, other domestic celebrations and every kind of festivity. At Pavan Pol they perform for an exclusively male audience whose members, if they wish, can engage the courtesans for more personal entertainment.

I had been aware of the courtesans since childhood, having watched them perform many times at various celebrations. At the age of sixteen I went with some school friends to Pavan Pol, a visit which left a lasting impression. Perhaps it was then that I first thought of recording this extraordinary place and the people who inhabit it. Some of the courtesans went there because it was the only way they had of making a living. The majority, however, were born at Pavan Pol, growing up in the community and following the tradition of their mothers, grandmothers and beyond, as their own daughters will. It is, perhaps, the only place in India where the birth of a baby girl, and future breadwinner, rather than a baby boy is celebrated. Some five thousand people live in this enclosed community in filthy, overcrowded tenements, but even at the time we made the film, there was a sense of a fading tradition, that the younger members had their sights set on the Bollywood film industry and more.

Pavan Pol is a private world, and it is unlikely any other filmmaker would have been given access to it, but the whole compound belonged to my old friend Karim Samar, so I assumed there would be no difficulties. But Karim was terrified by my suggestion. "Are you crazy?" was his response. "This is mafia-controlled, drug-ridden territory, and many of the clients are respectable married men who would not appreciate being seen on film. We could all be killed." "Never mind about that," I replied, "let's just do it. This world is a natural for film."

I assembled a crew and over the next few days we shot at Pavan Pol. I wanted to show the daily lives of the courtesans, so we filmed throughout the day from morning until night, when the slum is transformed into a magical place, almost like an opera set sparkling with lights and glitter and the illusion of glamour. I also filmed the performances, with girls as young as thirteen already accomplished practitioners of the courtesans' arts.

Before we began to film, I spent many, many evenings at Pavan Pol, talking to the women, listening to them, and getting to know them. It would have been easy to portray just a superficial account, but as a director I wanted to create a more substantial and compelling picture, and the only way to do that was to engage in dialogue with the subjects. And I didn't want the women to feel they were being exploited. I remember one lady who, judging by the way she spoke and conducted herself, must have come from a privileged background but had fallen on hard times. She spoke to me and answered my questions, but I could tell that she was disturbed at the prospect of being filmed. Although she made no objection, I chose not to film her.

Ruth and Jim saw the footage I had shot, and Ruth came up with a fictional story to weave into the film that centered on an unscrupulous rent col-

I direct Zohra Segal, one of the narrators of The Courtesans of Bombay *(1981), as cameraman Vishnu Mathur looks on.*

James Ivory

lector. I asked Karim, the real landlord, to play that part. Karim had been a very good actor in college, but he was now a respectable barrister with a young family, so he was torn between preserving his dignity and being in the limelight again. I wanted Saeed Jaffrey to play the part of an obsessive client, and the brilliant Zohra Segal, a veteran of Indian and international stage and film, to play the part of a retired courtesan who prepares her famous lime pickles as she explains the customs of Pavan Pol. We returned to Pavan Pol at the beginning of the following year to shoot the additional footage.

When Karim had warned me that we might be killed while we were filming at Pavan Pol, he was not exaggerating. The pimps who controlled access to the courtesans frequently pulled knives on each other as they tried to poach clients. Fistfights and beatings were commonplace, and the level of violence was so terrifying that at one point our sound recordist just fled the place. We eventually found him sitting in a café trying to settle his nerves with a Coca-Cola.

I was so disturbed by what I had seen while we were shooting the film that I asked Karim why he didn't try to improve the place and the appalling conditions where sometimes a dozen people shared one small room. Karim could do nothing about the pimps and the mafia and the drugs, but perhaps he could do something about repairing the buildings. Karim explained that the rents he charged the courtesans were insignificant, the equivalent of a few dollars a month, and because in Bombay the rent laws favor the tenants, he would be unable to increase the rent to take into account the cost of improvements.

Merchant Ivory's twenty-first anniversary would occur in 1983, and I wanted to celebrate with an Indian film. *Heat and Dust,* the novel Ruth had worked on for many years, had been published to great acclaim in 1975, winning the Booker Prize, Britain's top literary award. This was to be the film that would change our fortunes—and we almost didn't make it. At the time of the book's publication we were involved in so many other projects that I felt it would be unfair to Ruth to option the book when I couldn't see when or how we could fit it into our schedule.

So another producer stepped in and commissioned the English playwright David Mercer to write the screenplay. I remember raising an eyebrow when I heard that Omar Sharif and Glenda Jackson had been cast in the leading roles. However, and not unusually in films, the project never got off the ground and when the option expired, we got it, and Ruth provided a new adaptation. I saw *The Householder* and *Heat and Dust* as bookends holding together our first twenty-one years of filmmaking.

A dense and complex work, *Heat and Dust* tells two parallel stories set in the present and in the 1920s, interweaving the story of Olivia, the wife of a British administrator in India who has an affair with a nawab for whom she eventually leaves her husband, and that of Anne, Olivia's great-niece who comes to India, her experience there echoing Olivia's story.

The film practically cast itself: Shashi in his signature part as the nawab; Greta Scacchi as Olivia, her first screen role; Christopher Cazenove as her husband; and for the contemporary story, Julie Christie as Anne and Zakir

Christopher Cormack

The awkward meeting between Indian and English ladies on the colonial subcontinent.

Shashi Kapoor as the nawab of Khatm in Heat and Dust.

• • • • • • • •

Our experience in the opulent palaces of the maharajahs while shooting Autobiography of a Princess *inspired the banquet scene in* Heat and Dust, *the first of those trademark Merchant Ivory extravagant dinner parties.*

Christopher Cormack

Christopher Cormack

Hussain as her lover. Zakir is a musician, a distinguished tabla player, and he had never acted before, but I had seen him perform many times and noticed his extraordinary gift for communicating with audiences through both his vibrant musical interpretations and his endearing personality. Jim was a little doubtful, especially because Zakir's scenes would be with Julie Christie. He was right to be cautious, but Zakir proved perfect in the part. Julie Christie, of course, was unrivaled as the greatest screen star of that period, with a string of acclaimed performances and an Academy Award for her role in *Darling*. There is a slightly off-center and unpredictable quality to her, and that, perhaps, is what makes her so fascinating and surprising on screen. Just before we offered her *Heat and Dust* she was approached by Sidney Lumet to play opposite Paul Newman in *The Verdict*, a part that was vastly more high profile and lucrative than the one we offered her. It was no contest really, but much to our astonishment she chose to do our film instead.

We set up the production in England prior to going to India, and I knew that I would need an assistant to look after matters in London while I was away. I called Adrian Hodges, an acquaintance of mine at Screen International, the British film trade publication, who suggested I meet with Paul Bradley. I invited Paul, a very handsome young man, to have coffee with me at Fortnum & Mason, and I put the deal to him. "I have a job for you," I explained, "but there is no office." I no longer had access to the facilities of London Weekend Television or the National Film Finance Corporation or any of the other companies I invaded whenever a collaboration made that possible. "Here's what I suggest," I continued to Paul. "Get a large attaché case that can accommodate all the files and papers and other business relating to the film. Then work out of telephone booths." I still joke about how our first office in London was a telephone booth, but to this day Paul, who has been my executive producer for twenty-one years, has never got out of the habit of hauling a large attaché case—his portable office—wherever he goes. Little did Paul realize that it was his fate to be tied to us for a very long time. Despite the upheavals and uncertainties of working with Merchant Ivory, Paul, astonishingly, has managed to retain his boyish looks. And that is how we operated until John Murray, Ruth's publisher, took pity on us and offered a small space in his offices—a corner of the mail room, in fact—but it was enough for us.

The Byzantine complexity of financing *Heat and Dust* is something that still gives me nightmares, which is no great surprise because there was a point when I came dangerously close to losing the company I had spent twenty-one years establishing. Typically, I received whole volumes of rejection letters from financiers—one Hollywood studio returned the screenplay with a letter thanking us for submitting *Eat My Dust*—before securing the $2.2 million budget from various sources, including the Rank Organization; Roger Wingate of Curzon Film Distributors, who had done well with *The Europeans*; the newly formed Channel 4 television in London; and a number of private investors from India.

However, some of the private investors—and their money—mysteriously disappeared a week before we were due to begin shooting in Hyderabad, and Jim, Ruth and I sat in despair in Delhi, wondering what to do. Ruth suggested we call the whole thing off, but I knew I could never do that. Apart from every other consideration, how was I to tell Julie Christie that the film for which she had given up *The Verdict* was history? Instead, I proposed that we commence filming as scheduled and I would try to come up with something. Money, preferably.

By Indian standards Hyderabad is a modern city, having been established in 1590, and is probably best known for the fabulous jewels of inestimable value and unique dimensions that have been accumulated by the Hyderabad royal family, Tony Korner's close friends. The diamond mines at Golconda, five miles from the city, have produced some of the biggest rocks in the world, including the Hope diamond, the Orloff diamond of Catherine the Great and the British crown's Kohinoor diamond. There were times during shooting when I seriously considered taking a spade and digging around for a few diamonds myself.

With so many pressing matters to deal with, I had little time to attend to the practical and logistical details of filming, so I asked my brother-in-law Wahid Chowhan, who had a very successful waterproofing business in Bombay, if he would handle those aspects of the production. Wahid had absolutely no experience in the film business, so he was thrown in at the deep end, but he proved to be a very resourceful, adept and efficient collaborator. At such a fraught time it was a great relief to have his assistance.

We had been shooting for three weeks in Hyderabad when the money ran out, a moment I knew was coming and had been dreading. There was no money to pay the actors or the crew. They continued to work, largely because I had promised that we would shortly be receiving funds from the UK investors, but I knew I had to produce some money from somewhere pretty damn quick. I took the rushes to London to show Roger Wingate, who liked what he saw, and a small amount of money trickled in to pay the English crew. But when the unit came to leave Hyderabad for the next location in Kashmir, there was no money to pay the hotel bills, so the hotels impounded our cameras and equipment, effectively paralyzing the production. I was already in Kashmir with the art director Agnes Fernandez at that time, and asked Shashi to act as guarantor for the hotel bills.

I had been trying frantically to raise money in New York, London, Bombay and Hong Kong, so when a telegram arrived for me in Srinagar from a potential investor who was interested in putting up a million dollars, I was so excited I felt I already had the million dollars in my hands. I went to receive the cast and crew at the airport on their arrival from Hyderabad, and I showed Shashi the telegram. He looked suspicious and asked if the people were for real, or if I had forged the telegram. Neither: In the end that promise of a million just vanished.

Meanwhile, back in London, Roger Wingate was trying to put us into receivership because the film laboratory bills hadn't been paid, and we owed money all over the place. Paul Bradley was fending off telephone calls from a whole stream of creditors, and even Mrs. Leeston, Ruth's editor, was having to field angry calls: "I assure you that Mr. Merchant will honor all his debts, every last penny," she would announce in a firm tone at any inquiry that called into question my integrity. It was a desperate, desperate time—and it looked like the end of Merchant Ivory.

Michael White, an old friend and a very well-connected impressario and producer, arranged a meeting with Sir Jacob Rothschild of the prominent banking family, who viewed the edited film and liked it enough to offer a deal that would pay our debts and buy out Roger Wingate's investment. The deal was worth half a million pounds—all that stood between us and bankruptcy.

That incident didn't damage our relationship with Roger, who had been a great champion of our films since *Savages*. His actions were not prompted by any kind of malice, but by an understandable desire to protect his interests. He continued to invest in our films, and the mutual admiration and respect between us has been maintained over many years.

We screened the film at MIFED, the trade show in Milan where Rank gave a party for us. Greta had invited her father, an artist and noted art forger, and she was rather nervous about him seeing the film because she had a few nude scenes. She was only twenty-two then, and she thought her father might not approve. He didn't, and they had a row after the screening, but he thought the film was very beautiful and, of course, it made Greta a star. After the huge financial struggle of making the film, I felt vindicated by the number of offers from buyers at MIFED.

The film opened in London in February 1983 at the Curzon, Mayfair, where it ran for eleven months after receiving the best reviews we had ever had. In France it took in over a quarter of a million admissions, the biggest business we had ever done there, although we never saw any money beyond the initial advance because the French distributor went bankrupt. The film had been sold to Canal Plus, which saw no reason to pay us. In New York I had the thrill of seeing *Heat and Dust* running at the Paris cinema very successfully and *The Courtesans of Bombay* playing concurrently downtown.

The interest in India as a theme for film—something we had spent twenty years trying to cultivate—suddenly engaged both filmmakers and audiences.

In 1982 the multi–Academy Award winner *Gandhi* made a deep impact on audiences; *Heat and Dust* was followed by David Lean's *A Passage to India*; and the two massive television series *The Jewel in the Crown* and *The Far Pavilions* were produced—all very high profile and very successful internationally.

The publicity campaign for *Heat and Dust* was so huge that on the Sunday before it opened, three national newspapers in England—the *Sunday Times*, the *Sunday Telegraph* and the *Observer*—had the film featured on the covers of their magazine supplements. As far as I know, no other film has achieved this kind of publicity. Editors normally do not like to duplicate the stories run by their rivals. The three covers—of Madhur Jaffrey, Greta Scacchi and Julie Christie—were framed together and hung in our London office. It was just one room in Soho's Marshall Street, but it meant Paul now had a desk and a telephone. This sudden change in our fortunes brought with it the necessity for an accountant, so I engaged Sunil Kirparam, who somehow managed to keep track of our accounts despite the unpredictable nature of our finances. Like Paul, Sunil has been with us ever since, and is still trying to create order out of financial chaos, calmly juggling budgets and bank accounts and bills.

And I could also afford to buy a flat in London. London was an important center for us, and it was also a regular stop between New York and In-

Greta Scacchi as Olivia, a free-spirited English-woman in India in the 1920s.

Christopher Cormack

dia, so it made a lot of sense to establish a base there. I remember Jennifer Kendal coming to view the flat with me. She noticed it had a nice kitchen and dining room and she told me she looked forward to enjoying many, many meals with us. Alas, it was not to be. The following year Jennifer died of cancer. We had become so close over the years that I feel somehow she is still here, laughing and sharing the success we have achieved.

Heat and Dust marked a turning point in our lives. To mark our twenty-first anniversary, John Pym, then assistant editor of the film journal *Sight and Sound*, made a television documentary about us, *The Wandering Company*, which was shown on Channel 4, and he also wrote an accompanying book. In addition, a retrospective of our work was held at the National Film Theatre in London. All this was very exciting and gratifying, and meant more to me than producing a blockbuster that would be forgotten tomorrow.

By the time *Heat and Dust* opened, we were already in preproduction for *The Bostonians*, our second Henry James adaptation, which we shot in marvelous locations in Newport, Rhode Island and Martha's Vineyard in August 1983, with the financing again coming largely from England rather than America. *The Bostonians* gave us our first major Academy Award nomination—for Vanessa Redgrave as Best Actress—and we were all absolutely thrilled.

After the release of *The Europeans* in the spring of 1979, I took a holiday, the first in more than twenty years, and I haven't had one since. I traveled with Dick Robbins to the Greek island of Corfu, where we rented a small cottage and spent our time relaxing, eating and reading. One of the books I read was E. M. Forster's *A Room with a View*, which I enjoyed enormously.

Of all Forster's works, *A Passage to India* was, I imagine, the one we were expected to show interest in. There were all kinds of reasons why we decided against it, not least that Satyajit Ray had wanted to make it years earlier, but Forster had resisted all advances by filmmakers during his lifetime. When the rights became available after Forster's death, Ray decided not to make the film. By late in his career, Ray had had second thoughts. He did not feel that the main character, Dr. Aziz, rang true.

We chose to make *A Room with a View,* shooting in the spring of 1985 and releasing the film the following March. Like all our films it was small scale and small budget, so we were completely unprepared for the overwhelming reception it received from both audiences and critics. It opened on both sides of the Atlantic to universally ecstatic reviews, breaking box office records everywhere, and running at the Curzon, Mayfair, for a year. It was nominated for eight Academy Awards, and won three, to add to the vast number of other international awards it picked up. The film, which had cost $2.8 million to make, grossed over $60 million worldwide and, in the memorable words of one film commentator, catapulted us from the art house into the multiplex.

This was success on a scale that even I, in my wildest dreams, could not have imagined. What pleased me most was that we had achieved all this on our own terms and in our own way, without compromising the integrity of our work.

A Room with a View was chosen to open the Delhi Film Festival in January 1987, and I invited Helena Bonham Carter to join me there for the festivities. Helena is a very spirited young lady, always ready for an adventure, and she agreed to come even though she could only stay for twenty-four hours. Raj Kapoor, Shashi's brother, hosted a lunch in her honor that started at one o'clock in the afternoon and ended at five. Every kind of northern Indian speciality was prepared with the utmost delicacy and served with elegance. During the lunch, the Kapoor clan, four generations of them, fell madly in love with her. They refused to let Helena leave, and they tried everything they could to persuade her to stay in India and become a singing and dancing damsel in distress in Bollywood movies.

The most gratifying moment for me was visiting Satyajit Ray in his hotel suite after the screening of *A Room with a View.* He told me he was delighted with the film, and he was particularly impressed with the way we had shot the murder on the Piazza Signoria in Florence. There can never be a greater thrill than the approbation for your work from someone who is a master of that particular métier. In Ray's presence I always felt as I had when

The late Queen Mother greets me, James Ivory and Ruth Prawer Jhabvala at the London premiere of A Room with a View in 1985.

I showed him *The Householder*, hoping and seeking his approval. Seeing him beaming with appreciation at a film I had made was one of the most precious pleasures of my life.

There was also a sense of triumph when I showed my parents the reviews, and the box office results. They had been very supportive of my chosen career, although I know they would have preferred me to follow a more conventional profession. When I began making films, my father kept urging me to make action thrillers because there was money in them and no money at all, as far as my father could see, in classic art house films. For years he had been trying to steer me away from the kinds of films we were making toward more commercial material. I think my parents were terrified that the route I was taking would lead to me to penury, and they were so happy and excited, and probably relieved, when they saw the success of *A Room with a View.*

Of course the commercial success of *A Room with a View* immediately made us hugely interesting to the Hollywood film studios. Regarded by them with only bemused curiosity in the past, they now bombarded us with projects. But we went back to Forster and an adaptation of *Maurice,* a novel that had remained unpublished during the author's lifetime partly because he regarded it as an inferior work, but also because of its subject matter, which dealt with homosexuality. The Hollywood executives who had been courting us so relentlessly probably scratched their heads at the choice.

Other film producers might have capitalized on the success of *A Room with a View* by taking the Hollywood route. I went backward: to India, to pursue two projects that had been on my personal agenda for some time and that I was now in a position to execute. I had long wanted to organize an independent film unit in India to give the many talented people working in the industry there an opportunity to make modestly budgeted films for distribution in the West.

As far back as 1968 I had been interested in filming *The Perfect Murder,* from the novel by Harry Keating. The project had first been brought to my attention by the British stage director Jonathan Miller, who had been commissioned by Universal Pictures to write the screenplay. The studio chose not to pursue the project, so we bought the rights to make the film. I took on the role of executive producer, handing the responsibility for the production itself to my brother-in-law Wahid Chowhan, who, after his involvement in *Heat and Dust,* now wanted to be seriously involved in film. In many ways this ended up as a kind of family film: My young nephew Nayeem played a small role in the film, as did Madhur Jaffrey and her daughter Sakina. Madhur and Saeed had divorced many years earlier, but had produced three beautiful and talented daughters.

Neither Jim nor Ruth was particularly interested in this humorous detective story, and Jonathan Miller was no longer available. A new script was written by Keating himself, and I asked Zafar Hai to direct. Hai had made quite a name for himself in India as a director of documentaries and, more particularly, commercials—a vastly important and lucrative sector in India,

The charge of the British East India Company brigade in The Deceivers.

* * * * * * * * * *

Pierce Brosnan, as William Savage in his Thuggee disguise, abandons Merchant Ivory restraint.

where successful directors are treated with a huge amount of deference. This was Hai's first feature film and he was helped greatly by Walter Lassally, who photographed it. The film worked out well but, sadly, never found its audience despite compelling performances from Naseeruddin Shah, one of India's most accomplished actors, and the Swedish actor Stellen Skarsgard, who had been so memorable in Ingmar Bergman's *Hamlet.*

The other project I wanted to pursue was *The Deceivers,* from the John Masters novel based on the real-life exploits of William Sleeman, an Englishman in the Indian Political Service who disguised himself as an Indian to penetrate and destroy the Thuggees, a cult that ritually murdered and robbed travelers in the name of Kali, the goddess of destruction. I would finally be following my father's advice and making an action thriller, although I didn't know at the time that the term would apply as much to the making of the film as to the film itself.

The Deceivers gave me the opportunity of shooting in some of India's most exotic locations, places that I had wanted to explore but would have been unsuitable for our previous films. Our first location was Jaipur, the capital of Rajasthan and a city that dazzles with vibrant colors. Color is everywhere in

Mikki Ansin

Jaipur, from the pink sandstone of its rich architecture—which has given it its nickname the pink city—to the local multicolored dress of the women and the spectrum of shades that blaze in every street and bazaar. The whole place is like a painter's palette come to life. From there we went to the medieval city of Agra, dominated by India's greatest landmark, the Taj Mahal, and finally Khajuraho, a remote village, little known except to scholars and archaeologists who go there to study the thousand-year-old temples with their extraordinary erotic sculptures.

Mikki Ansin

Sadly, neither Jim nor Ruth shared my enthusiasm for this project: Jim felt the story was too violent for him, and Ruth thought that this kind of film would be better served by a male screenwriter. And so began the long trawl for a writer and director who could collaborate, which is no easy matter at all. The playwright Charles Wood was commissioned to write the screenplay, but when Marek Kanievska came on board to direct, he wanted significant changes to the script. By that time Wood had taken on other commitments and didn't have the time to work with Kanievska. So we commissioned another writer, but then Kanievska took on another project. The highly rated British director Stephen Frears agreed to step in, but he didn't like the screenplay, and wanted another writer to work with him. And on and on it went. David Lynch, Louis Malle, Costa-Gavras . . . the list of directors and writers who came and went just grew and grew, and a great deal of time and money was spent. Michael White, who was coproducing the film, and I had been carefully scrutinizing every director's suitability for this particular project, but we had reached the stage when we would have been delighted to hand it to anyone who was remotely interested in doing it. The American director Nick Meyer was interested, so he got the job, and a pre–James Bond Pierce Brosnan was cast in the leading role. With each change of director there had been a corresponding change of cast, each director having a firm idea of the kind of actor he wanted in the main parts, and I frequently wondered if this never-ending writer/director/cast-juggling act would ever be resolved.

We were exhausted even before we began shooting the film, and our problems hadn't even started. The line producer I had engaged for the film, an Englishman who clearly yearned for a return to the days of the Raj and the British domination of India, brought in a production team that shared that attitude. Unfortunately, I was away for much of this critical preproduction period. Our twenty-fifth anniversary was being honored with various tributes and receptions and retrospectives that I had to attend. By the time I arrived in India, battle lines had been drawn between my regular collaborators—Walter Lassally, Jenny Beaven and others who knew India and had established close relationships with their Indian colleagues—and the production department, whose members felt it was acceptable to refer to our Indian accountant as Sooty.

Even before I could deal with that potentially explosive problem, I had to take on the Indian movie mafia. Foreign film productions that came to India were targeted by these characters who would offer their services, claiming they could negotiate all kinds of concessions and permissions from the various ministries and other relevant parties, and generally make life easier for the production. They would then give key jobs to their associates, overcharge for everything and practice all kinds of scams. Foreigners ignorant of the procedures and costs of filmmaking in India were easy prey. But I wasn't a foreigner, and I had been making films in India before many of these unscrupulous characters had been born. Our previous films in India were on such a small scale that we were of no interest to this organization, but this production was a different matter. And because I refused to hire people I thought were questionable, life was made very difficult for us.

Complaints were made to the government by associates of these troublemakers that our film was presenting a distorted picture of Indian mythol-

ogy and culture, an absurd accusation because the cult of the Thuggees is a well-documented part of Indian history and, furthermore, the government of India had approved the script and granted us permission to shoot the film. We were then accused of filming, for inclusion in the film, a sati that had recently taken place in a nearby village. Sati, the practice of burning widows on their dead husbands' funeral pyres, is an explosive issue in India. Outlawed by the British administration in India, the custom, nevertheless, still persists in remote and poor areas of the country where an unsupported widow becomes an unwelcome burden on her dead husband's family.

There was a sati scene in our film, but the notion that we would even consider filming a real one was an absolute outrage. Nor would we have known about it. The practice is against the law and therefore practiced covertly, and only discovered after the fact. Nevertheless, a writ was issued against us in the civil court of Jaipur, and when that was dismissed by the court, things got really ugly. One of the female members of the mafia band claimed that I had sworn at her. This might seem a trivial matter, but in India swearing at a woman in public is a criminal offense that carries a two-year prison sentence.

I had never met the woman, so how it was possible that I had sworn at her was a mystery. Furthermore, at the time this alleged offense was to have

Nina Gupta in the controversial sati scene during the making of The Deceivers.

Naseeruddin Shah as Inspector Ghote and Stellen Skarsgard as Axel Svenson in The Perfect Murder.

• • • • • • • • •

Me with Parmeshwar Godrej, who became an investor in The Perfect Murder, *at the wedding of my sister Rukhsana.*

John Swope

taken place I was hundreds of miles from the scene of the crime. Nevertheless, the police came to our production office late one night to arrest me on charges of obscenity, creating a public nuisance and swearing at a woman. They were out of luck because I was on a train traveling from Delhi back to Jaipur, but they raided our offices in search of incriminating evidence. Although I was absent from this scene, a journalist covering the film for the British press was very much present, and the story made international headlines the following day, splashed on the pages of the London papers and those of the *New York Times.*

I had committed no crime, yet the law had to go through its due process, and I completed the film under a cloud of arrest warrants and court hearings. All the charges against me were ultimately dismissed when the matter went to the High Court, and those who had brought the charges were discredited. It had been an unpleasant experience and I was furious that so much time and energy and money had been wasted on a silly and spurious matter in a country with much graver concerns.

Nor was that an end of the legal matters connected with this film. We had sold the distribution rights to *The Deceivers,* along with two other films, to Russia on the basis that they would release the film in only about ten cinemas. We discovered that they were, in fact, showing it in a hundred places, so we refused to release the other two films to them. They brought a lawsuit against us for the sum of $24 million, which, they claimed, was the profit they were anticipating from the films we were now depriving them of. This amount made me smile because it was, at best, optimistic. Jim had sleepless nights, wondering how we would ever be able to pay that amount if the arbitrators found in the Russians' favor.

After months and months of complicated legal wranglings, the arbitrators decided that although the Russians had lost some revenue for which we were liable, the amount was forty thousand dollars. I could have appealed this decision, but I had spent so much time in courtrooms and legal offices and judges' chambers over this film that I just wanted to settle the matter and put it all behind me.

At home in London with one of my legendary meals.

• • • • • • • • •

Emma Thompson and me at the BAFTA awards, where she received Best Actress and I Best Picture for Howards End. *Emma would go on to win an Oscar for her performance.*

There would have been some compensation for all this anguish if the film had been successful, but that wasn't the case. The only positive element to emerge from the whole sorry business of *The Deceivers* was that it began my literary career. The publishers Viking in London had approached me on several occasions with the suggestion that I might like to write a book about my life, but I had always turned them down because I simply didn't have the time to write a book. Also, an independent film producer's life is really not very glamorous, and I couldn't imagine who would want to read about a succession of meetings with financiers, endless negotiations with agents and long days in the office trying to work out the logistics of a film shoot. But the experience of making *The Deceivers* provided material that I felt would be interesting, and should be recorded. Viking felt the same way and commissioned the book that was published in 1988 to some very warm reviews.

I hadn't expected anything more to come from this excursion into print,

but suddenly I was being asked by the *New York Times* to review books about India, the *Financial Times* in London wanted a big piece on the state of the British film industry, and other publishers wanted books about the Merchant Ivory operation. I discovered I had a whole new career. Since then I have written four more books, together with a number of newspaper and magazine articles, and a great many editors have aged prematurely as they anxiously await my manuscripts and copy, which, when juggled with the demands of filmmaking, are nearly always late.

Hullabaloo in Old Jeypore: The Making of The Deceivers wasn't, strictly speaking,

my first book. In 1986 I had published *Ismail Merchant's Indian Cuisine,* a book of my own recipes that Dick Robbins had persuaded me merited serious attention. By this time I had established quite a reputation for cooking, and friends were always asking for my recipes. The problem was that I never followed recipes or cataloged my own. I don't think I have ever weighed or measured or counted an ingredient in my life. So Dick undertook to follow me around—Boswell to my Johnson—and record all my activities in the kitchen. Whenever I grabbed a handful of one ingredient or another, Dick would remove it from my fist, carefully weigh it and record it for the book.

Our next films, the contemporary comedy *Slaves of New York* and *Mr. and Mrs. Bridge* with Paul Newman and Joanne Woodward, kept us in the United States, as did *The Ballad of the Sad Café,* from the Carson McCullers novel, which was directed by the British actor Simon Callow. Then we shifted to England again to film the third of our Forster adaptations, *Howards End.*

We were completely unprepared for the response to *Howards End,* which

*Me (right) with the
novelist Anita
Desai, whose novel
In Custody was
adapted into my
film.*

* * * * * * * *

*Shabana Azmi as
Imtiaz Begum, the
younger wife of the
Urdu poet Nur.*

eclipsed even the startling reception of *A Room with a View*. The critics went into unanimous raptures about the film, and for many months after its release tickets were like gold dust. Lines of people hoping for seats snaked around the cinemas where it played. Anthony Hopkins, Emma Thompson, Vanessa Redgrave, Helena Bonham Carter and almost everyone else connected with the film were nominated for awards in their category. They collected a truck-load of awards from the New York Film Critics, the Los Angeles Film Critics, the Film Critics Association, the National Society of Film Critics, the Golden Globes, the British Academy of Film and Television Arts and the Academy Awards, where nine nominations resulted in three Oscars, including Best Actress for Emma Thompson and Ruth's second screenwriting Oscar.

Howards End had cost $8 million; it grossed over $70 million. These are the kinds of figures that Hollywood studios find very attractive, so no one raised any objections to our next film, *The Remains of the Day*, an adaptation of Kazuo Ishiguro's Booker Prize–winning novel, even though the story—the unexpressed and unresolved love between the butler and the housekeeper of an English stately home—was scarcely the kind of material to set the pulses

Anna Kythreotis

of Hollywood executives racing. *That* only happened after the film opened, when it was more wildly successful than even *Howards End.* The verdict of the critics was that the film was flawless, and the box office receipts seemed to reflect that opinion. Once again the film and its personnel featured heavily in nominations for every award, including eight Oscars, but this time we were up against *Schindler's List,* so . . .

Derrick Santini

Nevertheless, two massive consecutive successes had put us at the top of the game: We were now regarded as serious players. Merchant Ivory had also passed the stage when I had to qualify our title with the explanatory "the makers of *A Room with a View.*" Merchant Ivory now had a universally recognizable identity to the extent that, much to my surprise, things entirely unrelated to cinema were described as "Merchant Ivory." We had become an adjective.

We had also become part of the movie establishment, but anyone expecting us to play the game according to conventional rules had seriously miscalculated. The success of our recent films inspired other filmmakers to concentrate on classic novels, and the cinema of the last decade is rich with period movies: Forster, Wharton, James and Austen were all adapted for the screen—but not by us—although so closely had we become associated with this genre that many people thought they were ours, and frequently congratulated me for them. Hollywood studios pressed money on us to do any films we wanted.

But my next project was regarded as eccentric even by my own unpredictable standards: an adaptation of Anita Desai's novel *In Custody,* which dealt with the subject of Urdu language and culture in India through the central character of an Urdu poet. And I wanted to make it in Urdu.

I had had no great desire to direct a feature film until I'd read this novel, but the subject was so close to my heart that I doubted I could be entirely objective about anyone else's interpretation of the material. I knew that if I were ever to direct a feature film, it would not be for the sake of the exercise, but because I cared very strongly about the themes involved. Urdu is my language and my culture, and I saw this film as an homage to my heritage.

Spoken by tens of millions, Urdu is a lyrical language of metaphor and symbolism, a language of poets and scholars. Unfortunately, in the political conflict between India's Hindus and Muslims, Urdu is perceived as the language of Muslims, and by its association with religion the language has become part of the political propaganda war. Urdu is not a religion; it is the language of a culture that was once shared by both Muslims and Hindus. Desai illustrates this common link brilliantly in the relationship between the two leading characters: the great Urdu poet, played by Shashi Kapoor, who is resigned to the loss of the language, and the diffident Hindu college lecturer, played by Om Puri, who is committed to its preservation.

I had known Anita Desai since the time of *The Householder*. She was a friend of Ruth's, and when Jim and I went to Calcutta to consult Ray on that film, Ruth arranged for us to stay with Anita's mother, Mrs. Toni Mazumdar, a wonderful German lady who had married a Bengali. I had asked Anita to write the screenplay from her novel; the screenplay was then translated into Urdu by Shahrukh Husain, who incorporated into the script various verses by the great Pakistani poet Faiz Ahmed Faiz.

Although the novel is set in Delhi, I chose to shoot the film in Bhopal. Bhopal is the state capital of Madhya Pradesh, which used to be a Muslim state, and Urdu is still widely spoken there. Located in an area of outstanding natural beauty and dominated by two picturesque lakes, the Moguls made this place a refuge for artists, poets and musicians, and that tradition is still maintained: Today Bhopal has the distinction of being one of the great centers of art and culture in the country.

All of this made it an entirely appropriate location for the film, but I had another reason for wanting to shoot it there. Bhopal is the site of the devas-

tating Union Carbide gas explosion, which in 1984 killed thousands who lived in the shadow of the plant and wrecked the lives and health of thousands of others who still remain without adequate compensation for their tragedy. It was also one of the cities hardest hit by the violence and arson that followed the destruction of the Ayodhya mosque by Hindu extremists in 1992. With no money for restoration, the city's imposing stately buildings and elegant monuments and mausoleums have been left to decay. As an exemplar of the collapse of a culture, Bhopal, sadly, is ideal.

For all that, I had an enduring romantic notion of Bhopal inspired by a photograph I had seen as an adolescent and which represented for me the beauty and refinement of the city before it was beset by so many tragedies. Friends of my family's in Bombay had a son who had married a girl from Bhopal, and the photograph that was so impressed on my memory was one of the bride and groom sitting in a boat on the lake, the girl offering the boy

Nur's funeral procession through the streets of Bhopal.

Derrick Santini

a perfect lotus flower. The image was simple and powerful, and I have never forgotten it.

Although I was advised not to shoot in Bhopal—the curfew imposed after the 1992 riots had only just been lifted, and the atmosphere was still volatile—after going there to scout locations, nothing in the world would have made me change my mind. The faded, crumbling grandeur of the architecture, the sense of decline—it just couldn't have been reproduced anywhere else.

To complement this very strong sense of culture and place, Loveleen Bains and Shahnaz Vahanvaty, who often assisted Jenny Beavan with costumes on our previous films, created some wonderful costumes that served the film brilliantly.

And I had asked Larry Pizer, who had shot *The Europeans* for us, to be my cinematographer. Always calm and quietly spoken, Larry was someone I trusted absolutely to interpret my ideas and at the same time prevent my beginner's mistakes. Although I had made a number of documentaries, a feature film was a more complex matter whose technical demands I had yet to master. I felt quite confident that I knew exactly how to handle the artistic and dramatic elements of filmmaking, but I was also aware—and still am—that in technical matters I am very much an undergraduate.

I shed fifteen pounds while making the film and, according to some, displayed a corresponding increase in artistic volatility. I cut scenes if I felt they weren't working, or suddenly adapted scenes to take advantage of an unusual location, a striking face, a new idea. Although I had been observing Jim at work for thirty years and have learned a lot from him, I have my own way of working that is different from his. Instead of being thrown by the unexpected elements that can occur during filming, I actively welcome them. I like the sense of spontaneity and surprise, and making *In Custody* was one of the most fulfilling experiences of my life.

The last days of shooting on *In Custody* coincided with *Holi*, the Hindu spring festival that is celebrated with great exuberance: brightly colored water and bombs of vivid powder dyes are flung about, and the flinging doesn't

Derrick Santini

With Paul Bradley, who runs the Merchant Ivory London office, is seen Richard Hawley.

❋ ❋ ❋ ❋ ❋ ❋ ❋ ❋

Om Puri and Anita Desai at Holi, *the Hindu spring festival, where participants are drenched in flower dye.*

Anna Kythreotis

My Passage from India

stop until everyone is completely drenched and resembles a Jackson Pollock painting. It is great fun and a little scary and, of course, the whole unit, myself included, joined in the celebrations. The dyes that are used are potent and tenacious, and many days passed before we were finally able to eradicate the livid purple and green marks from our faces.

Colin Leventhal and David Aukin of Channel 4, to whom we had sold the film, were rather taken by surprise when I screened the film for them and they realized it was in Urdu with subtitles. They had expected the film, like the novel, to be in English. But I felt that a film about an Urdu poet would ring false if the poetry were recited in English.

As soon as shooting was completed on *In Custody*, I returned to Delhi for the Indian premiere of *Howards End* at the International Festival in Delhi, which James Wilby and Vanessa Redgrave, who had given such moving performances in the film, agreed to attend. Vanessa is a very close personal friend, and I was touched by her loyalty in interrupting a particularly busy schedule to travel thousands of miles for this occasion. We arranged that they would arrive the day before the premiere, and Vanessa had to leave on the following day. But these careful calculations collapsed on the morning of their arrival when an accident at Delhi airport diverted their plane to Bombay. There was a typically Indian absence of information about when flights to Delhi would resume, and Vanessa and James spent the next twenty-four hours waiting at Bombay airport, finally arriving in Delhi the next morning just in time for the press conference.

Thousands of people had gathered outside the festival hall that evening, and Vanessa was reluctant to go inside unless she could take some of the crowd with her. The hall was already packed with invited guests and ticket holders, so because we were already running late, this was no time for one of Vanessa's admirable gestures. I told her, untruthfully, that the crowds were waiting for the next performance, and maneuvered her into the cinema. We had a long and busy night ahead: a recital by Zakir Hussain and his ensemble, and then a moonlit visit to Saint Nizamuddin's shrine, where we were besieged by beggars waiting for alms (because this was a celebration, I fol-

Berliner Studio

At the premiere of The Remains of the Day, *where we first heard the phrase "Gold-Ismail" from the photographer's command, "Goldie, smile!"*

lowed the custom of paying a local restaurant to feed them all). It was not until dinner, after forty-eight hours without sleep, that Vanessa began to flag, intoxicated by the dizzying incense from the shrine and by Zakir's music, which she described as "angels coming from heaven to perform for us." At dawn she flew off to Rome to resume her work.

When *In Custody* opened at the Liberty cinema in Bombay, I invited Goldie Hawn to accompany me to the premiere. I had come to know Goldie extremely well after escorting her to the opening of *The Remains of the Day* in Los Angeles, and I have always enjoyed her lively and charming company. Goldie has a great fascination with Indian mysticism and culture. She was planning to produce a film in Pakistan and had asked me to coproduce it for Disney, but sadly, the film was never made, though we have remained close. She brought with her Sally Field, who was going through a difficult patch in her life, so I was escorted by two Hollywood legends on that occasion.

The guest of honor that evening was Nimmi. My infatuation with her had never really diminished with the years, and she enchanted me now as much as she had always done. At the end of the screening she spoke to me in Urdu, and there were tears in her eyes as she complimented me on my film. She had known me as a besotted kid, and now she was seeing me as a grown man who had accomplished his dreams. It was a very moving moment for me, and one that I will always remember and cherish. The crowds threw

Me and composer Richard Robbins, who has worked with Merchant Ivory for more than twenty-five years, on location in Paris.

marigolds as we came out of the cinema, just as they had done on the night that had shaped my future.

Soon after I had finished shooting *In Custody*, Dick Robbins came to Bombay to complete *Street Musicians of Bombay*, a documentary film he had begun some seven years earlier and had worked on intermittently since. The inspiration for the film came about on Dick's first trip to India in 1977. He was staying at the Taj Hotel, and awoke one morning to the sound of an ethereal duet being sung on the street below. The two singers, a leper couple, were part of Bombay's subculture of street entertainers: thousands of people who earn their livelihood by performing on the pavements of the city. What most visitors to India fail to understand is that the majority of these street folk are not beggars unable to earn a living any other way, but traditional performers who follow the practices of their fathers and grandfa-

thers and great-grandfathers: They are monkey wallahs and bear wallahs, tightrope walkers and magicians, snake charmers and acrobats.

But by far the largest group of these itinerant players are the musicians, and counted among these singers and instrumentalists are the *hijrahs*, who continue yet another ancient tradition. The hijrahs are castrated men, and hermaphrodites, who live and dress as women and are outcasts from conventional society but, paradoxically, serve an important function within it. Their appearance at celebrations such as weddings and childbirth, even at the highest levels of society, is considered a good omen. They can be abusive and throw curses if they are not rewarded as generously as they expect, but their behavior is always tolerated either because of superstition or because in ancient times they were a fixture at the courts of the maharajahs, where they sang and danced, and even instructed the young royals in etiquette.

All this fascinated Dick, and as a musician he was particularly intrigued by the variety of instruments, the voices, the whole musical spectacle. We had shown aspects of this culture in all our Indian films, but no one had ever explored the subject in any depth. Dick wanted to put these musicians on film as a matter of record before they disappeared from the urban landscape, something which was already beginning to happen. I encouraged him to pursue the idea, and gradually what had begun as an anthropological exercise developed into a vibrant and engaging documentary that was financed by Channel 4 Television in London and was extremely well received when it was broadcast.

It would be several years before I worked in India again. In 1994 we were based in Paris making a bunch of Gallic-themed films that will probably become known as Merchant Ivory's French Period: *Jefferson in Paris*, about the American statesman's time as ambassador to France; *Surviving Picasso*, a portrait of the artist and the women who shared his life; *A Soldier's Daughter Never Cries*, from Kaylie Jones's semiautobiographical novel about her father, the

With my nephew
Nayeem Hafizka on
the set of The
Proprietor.

noted American novelist James Jones; and *The Proprietor*. But even then, India was never really out of the picture: Most of the costumes for *Jefferson in Paris* were made in India, which not only has some of the finest tailors for creating period costumes, but also skilled craftsmen who can reproduce authentic fabrics.

With our activities concentrated in Paris, we opened the fourth Merchant Ivory office there, and I was delighted that my niece Rahila Bootwalla, the daughter of my sister Rashida, became the co-*jiroux*, helping me with the productions and accounting. She also become a French citizen. My own relationship with France was sealed in 1997 when the French government awarded me its principal cultural honor, *Commandre d'Ordre des Artes et Lettres*, in recognition of our contribution to cinema.

I also bought an apartment in Paris that ultimately became the set for *The Proprietor*, the second film I directed. I had had no plans to direct another feature until I met the legendary actress Jeanne Moreau at a party given by the

Indian ambassador in Paris to celebrate the opening of *In Custody* in France, and was inspired to create a film for her.

And I hadn't planned to direct a third film until Madhur Jaffrey brought to my attention *Cotton Mary*, a play written by Alexandra Viets that deals with the thorny issue of Anglo-Indians. A product of liaisons between the British administrators in India and the indigenous inhabitants, Anglo-Indians are spurned by both communities, regarded as neither Indian nor British.

Madhur wanted to play the lead role, an Anglo-Indian nurse who gradually assumes the identity of her British employers. She also wanted to direct the film, and that's where the problems began. Madhur had never directed a film before, but she is an experienced and gifted actress, and I had no doubt she was up to the task. Unfortunately, the various financiers whom I approached for investment didn't share my confidence; they felt that it was too much for a novice director who was also expected to act in practically every scene. David Aukin of Channel 4 suggested he might be interested in getting involved but only if I were to direct. I wasn't very keen on this arrangement, not because I didn't want to work on the film, but because I knew how passionate Madhur was about directing it. When Universal Pictures came up with the same proposition, I realized that it was a choice between directing the picture myself or not making it at all. Madhur, understandably, was very upset by this development and wouldn't speak to me. And this in turn upset me because Madhur and I have been close friends for more than forty years, and it would be sad to have a film come between us.

I knew Madhur was unhappy, but we needed to communicate in order to resolve the problem. There were arguments and discussions, and finally Madhur decided that she was too old for the part of Cotton Mary and didn't want to play it. Her daughter Sakina, who was also in the film, eventually persuaded her that it was too good a role to turn down, and Madhur finally accepted the compromise by agreeing to a codirector credit.

There was another disappointment when Natasha Richardson, Vanessa Redgrave's daughter, whom I had been courting for over a year to play the part of the English memsahib, decided at the last moment not to do it be-

With Madhur Jaffrey, directing Cotton Mary *on location in Kerala.*

Seth Rubin

cause she was worried about the possibility of her children becoming sick in India. I contacted Greta Scacchi, who, fortunately, didn't share Natasha's qualms about bringing her children to India. Greta had given birth to a baby boy just six months earlier, and because the story involved a baby, she and her son would be perfect in the film.

But we also needed to find a newborn baby, fair-haired and pale skinned like Greta, and that was no simple matter in India. We contacted a doctor in a maternity hospital in Cochin, our principal location, and he allowed us to visit the new mothers to see if any of their babies were suitable. But the mothers were very suspicious of us; one mother shrieked and yelled when we entered her room, certain we were going to abduct her child. Eventually we found the perfect one, three days old and as quiet as a little mouse. The mother allowed us to take her baby which, like all great stars, came with a retinue—her grandmother, her hospital nurse and her doctor.

The baby behaved impeccably—in other words, she slept—until we came to shoot the scene that involved putting the baby on scales to be weighed. Whether it was the blazing lights, or the general noise and confusion that reigns on a film set, this peaceful little infant suddenly started yelling and screaming. I was terrified. I thought something terrible had happened to her.

That wasn't the end of the baby saga. We needed three more in various stages of development, so we had to go through the nightmare of finding appropriately aged babies, persuading their mothers that we were not baby snatchers, and then dealing with the shooting: As a rule, babies do not make cooperative actors, and they never pay any attention to their directors. It was a great relief when we were finally able to use Greta's baby.

We shot the film in Kerala, at the southernmost tip of India on the Malabar Coast, a picturesque region of sandy beaches, palm trees, labyrinthine canals, dense forests and tea plantations. It is probably India's most cosmopolitan region: Phoenicians, Arabs, Jews, Chinese and Europeans, particularly the Portuguese and Dutch, have all staked a claim there and left something of their culture and their religion behind, hence the confusion for the visitor confronted with Christian churches alongside Chinese pagodas and Jewish synagogues (the oldest synagogue in Asia is in the town of Cochin). What an ideal place, I thought when I first saw it, to suggest the confused identity of the Anglo-Indians in the story.

Because I dislike staying in hotels for long periods, I rented a house and invited lots of friends to visit. Jim, who was busy preparing for our next film, *The Golden Bowl*, came to Cochin for Christmas and helped me with the film, and I invited Shashi to come down from Bombay. I had arranged for *Heat and Dust* to be shown at a local cinema because it had never been seen in Cochin, and since Greta and Madhur were already there, I thought it might be fun to have a reunion.

The French cinematographer Pierre Lhomme, who had shot many of our films, was very enthusiastic when I approached him about photographing *Cotton Mary*. He had been in Cochin in 1956 to make a documentary and was eager to return and see the place again. As usual, I called on many members of our regular team. Richard Hawley, who had worked on a number of Merchant Ivory films in the past and now handles our affairs in New York, proved to be a tremendously reliable first assistant director. And my nephew

Rizwan, Wahid Chowhan's son, cut his filmmaking teeth on this film as my fourth assistant director. Over the years, the actors and technicians who have worked with us repeatedly have become known as the Merchant Ivory family. Gradually, many members of my real family have also been inducted into the business, and I have come to grow more and more reliant on their help.

I had also rented a house for Greta and her family, and I took the precaution of making sure it was within walking distance of our main locations. This was convenient for Greta because she was still breast-feeding her baby and needed to return home frequently during the day. And it also suited me because under this arrangement I could keep her under surveillance at all times and, more to the point, she could hear me yelling for her if she was late coming back to the set. There was no escape for Greta. But my Machiavel-

Seth Rubin

lian scheming almost went adrift when Greta's partner saw a snake on the road outside their house one day and insisted on moving from there. This would have been very inconvenient and disruptive, so I convinced him that the snake he had seen was, in fact, from a nonpoisonous variety, which, according to Indian myth, was there to protect the house. There *is* such a myth, but I had no idea whether the snake was the correct one.

Seth Rubin

The pacifist elephant who refused to destroy a village, on location for Cotton Mary.

Lily (Greta Scacchi) and John (James Wilby) in the garden of their colonial mansion.

One scene in the film involved a wild elephant going mad and destroying a village. We had been assured that the elephant engaged for this sequence would obey all orders and crush everything in its path. A village was built by the river, and we had set the scene up with dozens of extras who would run in panic from the village when the elephant rampaged. But the elephant just stood there. Another elephant had to be fetched, this one so aggressive that the mahout insisted on keeping it attached to a chain. By the time we finally captured the sequence on film, I was so tired and so hot that I just stripped down and fell into the river, lying there like a water buffalo. And after all that effort, the scene was cut from the film during the editing because it just didn't add anything to the story.

The film was savaged by the critics and avoided by audiences everywhere except, curiously, in Canada, where it received very good reviews and did well in the cinemas. In India, the release of the film resembled some rock band tour as I took my team, which included actors James Wilby and Madeleine Potter, writer Tama Janowitz and the blues singer Nell Carter, who played opposite Jeanne Moreau in my film *The Proprietor*, on a whirlwind journey of premieres and receptions and parties from Bombay to Delhi to Bangalore. This band—the Merchant Ivory groupies—were all connected in some way with our films. The American ambassador gave a reception for us at Roosevelt House in Delhi, where Nell Carter sang Gershwin and a few numbers from her Broadway show *Ain't Misbehavin'*. I'm sure Roosevelt House will never be the same after being shaken to its foundations by the extraordinary atmosphere generated by this enormous, brilliant black singer.

At the press conference, however, someone objected to the subject of the film, and the protests escalated until demonstrators succeeded in closing down the film in Cochin. We were accused of maligning and misrepresenting the Anglo-Indian community, which surprised me. Cochin has a large Anglo-Indian community, and we had used many of its members, both professional actors and ordinary people, in the film and no one had voiced any objection to the material either before or during the shooting.

I understand that this is a subject many Indians still feel sensitive about, and one of the problems of dealing with such issues is that they inevitably raise controversy. But one can't ignore something just because the facts are unpalatable. We experienced a similar situation with *Jefferson in Paris* because, although we showed a sympathetic portrait of the statesman, we did not ignore his relationship with Sally Hemmings, the black slave by whom he fathered a number of children.

A film that I had been eager to direct for six years was *The Mystic Masseur*, from the novel by V. S. Naipaul, regarded by many as the finest living writer in the English language. I knew from the beginning that getting Naipaul to agree would be hard work. Only Francis Ford Coppola has ever come close to getting the rights to one of his books—until Naipaul changed his mind and tore up the contracts.

Naipaul's American agent was then Andrew Wylie, otherwise known as The Jackal. I got nowhere with him. I then approached Naipaul's British agent, Gillon Aitken, a very proper and correct Englishman who very politely turned down my request in a tone that implied the matter was now at an end and should not be raised again. So I wrote to Naipaul himself, sug-

Mikki Ansin

Ayesha Dharker as Leela, Ganesh's wife, in The Mystic Masseur.

gesting I go to see him. Naipaul had met me several times in the 1960s and 1970s and knew of my single-minded approach. He wrote back urging me to stay away. He said he knew my persuasive powers were legendary, and he granted me the rights to *The Mystic Masseur,* asking me to work out the details with Gillon Aitken.

Set among Trinidad's Indian community in the 1940s, *The Mystic Masseur,* Naipaul's first novel, is a delightful satire about the meteoric and bewildering rise of a young man named Ganesh from failed schoolteacher and incompetent masseur, to author, revered mystic and politician who is finally awarded the MBE by the British government. When I read the book, I enjoyed it so much, laughed so much and became so absorbed with the roguish, crazy characters that I felt audiences would react in the same way.

I asked Caryl Phillips to write the screenplay, unaware that Naipaul would not be keen on my choice. Naipaul had reservations that Phillips, a West Indian from the island of St. Kitts, would be unfamiliar with Indian customs and traditions, and would fail to connect with Indian sensibilities. By the time Naipaul had raised his objections and presented me with his choice of writer, Phillips had already written an admirable script, and I felt committed

to it. The situation grew worse when Phillips published an article in an American journal that was critical of Naipaul's work. I have a great respect and admiration for Naipaul as a writer, and the fact that he was awarded the Nobel Prize in Literature in 2001 speaks for itself. No one could have cheered more loudly than I did when I heard that news. Phillips, however, is entitled to his own opinion and has the right to express it.

Soon after I acquired the rights to the book, and long before I had even begun to think about casting, I went to see a one-man play in New York called *Sakina's Restaurant*, which had received glowing reviews, particularly for its performer Aasif Mandvi, who played all six roles, both male and female. As I watched him segue from one character to the next, I knew I had found the actor to play the lead in the film. I went to see him backstage after the show and asked if he would be interested. There was no script at that point, so I suggested he read the book. I think he was rather surprised to be

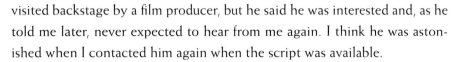

visited backstage by a film producer, but he said he was interested and, as he told me later, never expected to hear from me again. I think he was astonished when I contacted him again when the script was available.

The novel was so entertaining and enjoyable and the characters so rich that I wasn't in the least surprised when nobody wanted to invest in the film. Today more than ever, films are so conventional and formulaic that no one wants to take a risk on something out of the ordinary. "Who wants to see a film about a bunch of Indians in Trinidad?" was the standard response to a film that was about a great deal more than that for anyone who troubled to look.

The financing finally came from private investors in India and Trinidad, sourced by my nephew Nayeem Hafizka, who graduated with honors as a film producer on this film. The son of my third sister, Safia, Nayeem began his career as a runner on *A Room with a View*. A runner is poorly paid (sometimes even unpaid), expected to do everything for everybody, know everything, anticipate everything, be put upon by everybody and take the blame when things go wrong. Now that I think about it, that is also the perfect description of a film producer. When Nayeem first told me he wanted to work in the movies, I advised him to watch me and learn. Now I watch him wheeling and dealing, hustling and bustling, and I'm very proud of him.

Among the many Merchant Ivory regulars reunited on this film was the actress Zohra Segal, a veteran of almost every Anglo-Indian film who is as busy at the age of eighty-eight as she has always been. In deference to her age and apparent frailty, I assigned a member of the crew to act as her guardian, escorting her to and from the set, shielding her from the sun with an umbrella, bringing her cool drinks and generally making the laborious process of filming more comfortable for her. Never has my concern been more misplaced. "In my last film I played a karate-fighting biker in full leather gear," I overheard her whispering gleefully to someone. "Don't tell Ismail."

Over the past forty years of filmmaking I have never lost sight of the debt I owe to Satyajit Ray, nor have I ever forgotten the manner with which he responded to our requests for help. Ray's endorsement early in our careers gave us the confidence to continue, and he set the example I wanted to follow as soon as I was able. In 1991 we established the nonprofit Merchant Ivory Foundation on part of Jim's farm in Claverack. Conceived initially as a film center where workshops in all aspects of independent filmmaking could be held, with the participants housed in the various small properties on the farm, the activities have expanded to include art exhibitions and concerts. Most important, perhaps, the foundation also awards grants for the development or completion of promising independent films. The first project of the foundation was to restore Ray's films.

At about this time I learned that Ray, who suffered from a heart condition, was declining in health. I felt it was time for him to be recognized for his important contribution to cinema by the Academy of Motion Picture Arts and Sciences, which had never honored him. I got in touch with Martin Scorsese, who I knew shared my admiration for Ray, and suggested we should lobby the Academy. Scorsese and I drafted a letter that was sent to Academy members petitioning their support. The response was overwhelming and extraordinary. Fellini, Kubrick, Lucas, Coppola, Zeffirelli, Kurosawa, Paul Newman, Anthony Hopkins, Dustin Hoffman, Woody Allen were just a few of the movie luminaries who unreservedly endorsed our proposal. Among the many hundreds of those letters and testimonials written to the Academy's board of governors, that of Gregory Peck made a significant point:

> With the current U.S. preoccupation with weekly box office figures, projected to the press and the TV audience like football scores, the image of our industry is that box office figures are our sole measure of success.

Mikki Ansin

By honouring Satyajit Ray, the Academy would not only honour a true artist in film, it would remind the public and the media once more that Academy Awards are given for artists' excellence.

Indian culture in the new world: a dancer at the wedding of Ganesh and Leela in Trinidad, from The Mystic Masseur.

Ray was elected as the recipient of the Lifetime Achievement Award in 1992. As soon as the announcement was made, I telephoned him in Calcutta to offer my congratulations. He was thrilled with the award, and told me it was the greatest honor he had ever received. I was so pleased to hear that it had made him so happy, and that I had played a part in that. Then he stunned me by saying, "I don't know how people in Hollywood even know or remember me." I told him I would be sending him a package and he could judge for himself how his work was appreciated. I collected some of the letters that had been written to the Academy—the most glowing endorsements from

Elia Kazan, Billy Wilder, Robert De Niro and others—and sent them to Ray. He was too ill to attend the Academy Awards ceremony, so Audrey Hepburn presented him with his Oscar for Lifetime Achievement via satellite. He died a month later.

Richard Schickel, who was responsible for producing the televised tribute to Ray as part of the Oscar ceremony, contacted me about getting some footage of Ray's films to show on the film. I was horrified to discover that the negatives of the films that were stored in India had deteriorated badly, and that his entire body of work was on the point of vanishing.

I contacted the Academy of Motion Pictures Arts and Sciences, which agreed to supervise the restoration of nine of Ray's films, and we raised the money through the Merchant Ivory Foundation. I managed to obtain the negatives to six of the films in India, and had them sent to the Henderson Film Laboratory in London. In the spring of 1993 the laboratory burned down in a nitrate film explosion, and the Ray films were almost entirely destroyed. It was devastating news.

After rescuing what was left of those burned negatives, we immediately set about trying to obtain duplicate negatives, interpositives and release prints* from a number of sources, including the Indian National Film Archives, the British Film Institute, the Museum of Modern Art in New York and various international film archives. All the original negatives we sourced were badly damaged by dirt and scratches, and had deteriorated in the heat and humidity of the Indian climate. But by using the best of the material we had, and taking advantage of the latest technology and restoration techniques, the Film Technology Company in Los Angeles managed to create new master copies of the films. The soundtracks of these films went through a similar process with the latest advances in digital audio restoration. Nine of Ray's films went through this process, at a cost of almost a million dollars, and the results were nothing short of miraculous. The successful restoration was a great comfort after the shocking incident at Henderson's Laboratory.

*Interpositives are an intermediate stage between a negative and a new negative. A release print is what goes out to the theaters.

The purpose of restoring these films was to save and preserve Ray's legacy, but once that was done, and done so successfully, I felt the films should be seen. A whole generation had never had the chance to experience these masterpieces. I acquired the rights to the films from the National Film Development Corporation in India, and then persuaded Sony Classics to distribute them in the form of a national tour of major cities in the United States and, subsequently, to make them available on videocassette.

While the international film community applauded our efforts in this matter, the National Film Development Corporation chose to sue us. We were accused of deliberately burning the negatives as an act of envy or revenge on Ray, and exploiting his films from which we had made millions of dollars. These accusations were as wide of the mark as they were painful. I had accepted this massive undertaking as a gesture of love, respect and, above all, loyalty to Ray, and I was bitterly and profoundly hurt. No one who truly loves film could ever contemplate destroying the works of Ray or all the other classics that were lost in the blaze. The cost of restoring his films far outweighed any revenue they might earn, and profit was never the motive for this pursuit. The court procedures are such that they may drag on forever.

With Rahila Bootwala.

It has been a long, arduous and often impossibly difficult effort to obtain what fragments I could of Ray's films from around the world, to raise the money for the restoration, and then ensure that the results would stand as a memorial for all time to his work. But never for a moment have I regretted taking on the task.

Just as I was coming to the end of writing this book, I learned that Ruth, Jim and I were to receive the Fellowship of the British Academy of Film and Television Arts, the highest award in British film, to add to the

award Merchant Ivory had been given last year by the New York State Council on the Arts for our cultural contribution to the performing arts. We were absolutely thrilled, and immensely gratified that our work was being recognized in this way.

After receiving many honors and tributes internationally, only an honor from India was missing. Every year on Republic Day, January twenty-sixth, the president of India bestows honors on people of distinction in different fields, and at the beginning of this year I received a telephone call from India advising me, in the strictest confidence until the formal announcement could be made, that I was to receive *Padma Bhusan*, the equivalent of a British knighthood.

Receiving Padma Bhusan, *one of the highest honors bestowed by the Indian government, from Shri K. R. Narayanan, president of India.*

From left, James
Ivory, Helena
Bonham Carter,
Ruth Prawer
Jhabvala, Vanessa
Redgrave and me.
The Merchant
Ivory triumvirate
received a BAFTA
Fellowship, the
British Academy's
highest award, in
2002.

The ceremony took place on March 27, 2002, at Rashtrapati Bhavan, the magnificent Presidential Palace. Dressed in a traditional flowing kurta and shawl, I felt I was in a scene from an Indian miniature painting. Among the twenty-eight recipients was my friend and collaborator Zakir Hussain, and I was so happy to see him receive his honor. When my moment came, I walked up to accept the citation and the gold insignia of *Padma Bhusan* from the president of India. He said he felt honored to present me with the award, and he had been delighted by the consistent quality of the films we had made. This was a ceremony rooted in history and, for me, it represented a reality absent from the glitz and glamour of show business awards whose artificial tone paled beside the dignity of this occasion.

After the ceremony my sister Rukhsana had tears in her eyes as she embraced me. "If only our parents had been alive to see this," she said. It was a thrilling moment for the boy from Bombay whose only dream had been to make movies.

Unlike Ganesh, *The Mystic Masseur* of my film, who, after a life full of in-

cident, collects his MBE from the British government and settles into a happy retirement, this is not my final chapter.

For me, the possibility of retirement seems to grow more remote as the projects keep coming. At a party in New York to celebrate my *Padma Bhusan*, Matthew Modine, one of the stars in our latest film, *Le Divorce*, gave me a small, elegantly wrapped gift: a copy of *Jacob's Hand*, written by Aldous Huxley and Christopher Isherwood. Matthew had been moved by the book, and thought it would make a fine film that we might collaborate on. What Matthew didn't know was that I had a connection with these writers. I had met the tall, imposing Huxley in Los Angeles in 1960, when he came to lecture at the University of California, and we had talked about my film *Creation of Woman*, along with other Indian myths and philosophies. At about the same time I also met Christopher Isherwood, who was living in Los Angeles and had a guru at the Vedanta Center. My friendship with Huxley and Isherwood continued over the years, and in the early 1980s Jim and I tried to make a documentary about Isherwood and his book *October*. Published in 1983, this was a fascinating work that recorded his life on each day of that month. But in 1986, while we were still struggling to find funding, Isherwood died, and I have always regretted losing the chance to make that film.

With Zakir Hussain at a reception celebrating Padma Bhusan *at home in Bombay.*

Now Matthew, unknowingly, was reviving my connection with the two writers, which made his proposal hard to ignore. Of such encounters and miracles has our destiny been shaped.

That book has now joined the huge pile of scripts and other literature waiting for attention. And the Merchant Ivory adventure continues, I hope, for another forty years.

The three of us.